Brimming with creative inspiration, how-to projects, and useful information to enrich your everyday life, Quarto Knows is a favorite destination for those pursuing their interests and passions. Visit our site and dig deeper with our books into your area of interest: Quarto Creates, Quarto Cooks, Quarto Homes, Quarto Lives, Quarto Drives, Quarto Explores, Quarto Gifts, or Quarto Kids.

10 9 8 7 6 5 4 3 2

ISBN: 978-1-59186-692-3

Library of Congress Cataloging-in-Publication Data

Names: Balz, Michelle, author.
Title: Composting for a new generation: latest techniques for the bin and beyond / Michelle Balz; photography by Anna Stockton.
Description: Minneapolis, MN: Cool Springs Press, 2018. | Includes bibliographical references.
Identifiers: LCCN 2017025810 | ISBN 9781591866923 (sc)
Subjects: LCSH: Compost.
Classification: LCC S661 .B356 2018 | DDC 631.8/75--dc23
LC record available at https://lccn.loc.gov/2017025810

Acquiring Editor: Jeff Serena
Project Manager: Alyssa Bluhm
Art Director: Cindy Samargia Laun
Cover and Page Design: Evelin Kasikov
Photography: Anna Stockton;
    pages 47, 63, 85 (top), 152 © Shutterstock
Illustration: Bill Kersey; opening chapter illustrations
    by Evelin Kasikov

Printed in China

COMPOSTING FOR A NEW GENERATION

Latest Techniques for the Bin and Beyond

Michelle Balz

Photography by
Anna Stockton

COOL
SPRINGS
PRESS

Introduction

My name is Michelle, and I'm a compost fanatic. I'm not the only one. In fact, we're everywhere. I run into people all the time who tell me how they're obsessed with backyard composting. We're compost evangelists who spread our composting love to friends, family, and neighbors. When one of us encounters another composter at a party, we light up and spend the next hour talking about what kind of compost bin we have and swapping tips and tricks.

I cannot imagine life without composting.

When I'm on vacation and eat a banana, the mere act of dropping that banana peel into the trash actually hurts. So much potential lost to another landfill. While out running errands, I've been known to wrap apples cores in napkins and stash them in my purse so I can compost them at home. When looking at a bucket of potato peels or a bag of leaves, I see what they could become through composting: a rich, crumbly, dark-brown soil amendment full of beneficial organisms that will bring my soil to life.

Backyard composting isn't new. George Washington had a compost pile at Mount Vernon. Ancient Mesopotamian clay tablets refer to the use of manure, and there's evidence that many other ancient cultures—Romans, Greeks, Arabs—knew about composting. But mix human ingenuity with millions of people practicing backyard composting and you end up with fresh ideas, new gadgets, easier methods, and modern innovations to better fit our busy lifestyles. These techniques allow us to compost in our backyards without the smelly, stinky mess sometimes associated with decomposition.

The pages that follow describe modern advances in the backyard composting world while also covering time-tested techniques and expert advice.

Successful backyard composting starts with the basics, and this book includes everything beginners need to get started. More experienced composters will discover new concepts and inspiration to expand their composting horizons and create even more wonderful compost. Backyard composting can take as much or as little effort as you want to put in, but know that you will not be doing the work alone. Millions of your closest composting buddies have your back and will be with you from beginning to end.

Backyard composters embrace the do-it-yourself ethos. We take materials that would otherwise be garbage and turn them into a valuable soil amendment prized by home gardeners. Many composters continue that innovation and reuse or repurpose materials to build their own composting units. In the spirit of DIY, this book provides step-by-step instructions to create your own tools, recipes, and composting bins.

Some people install solar panels or raise backyard chickens to help the planet and gain a little more control over their lives. Backyard composting is our way of living "off the grid." We don't need bagged compost and overpriced fertilizers. We create life from death, beauty from rot. **We are composters.**

1

THE EXPECTED
AND UNEXPECTED
BENEFITS OF
COMPOSTING

WHY COMPOST?

Imagine taking materials that many people view as garbage and transforming them into something useful. When you compost, you create something that will amend your soil and improve your garden. You create something that has the ability to bind heavy metals so your plants won't absorb them. You create something that reduces your need for fertilizers and pesticides. Best of all, creating this special something requires no electricity, and you can make all the tools you need yourself.

Compost holds a special place in the hearts of serious gardeners as the most important soil amendment around. But aside from the many personal benefits you reap from composting, your decision to compost also benefits the world around you, positively affecting larger environmental issues. You win, your soil wins, and the planet wins.

Now, before we dive into the benefits of compost, let's consider what backyard composting means.

A Quick Primer

When you plant a garden, you control (or try to control) which plants grow and where they grow. When you compost, you attempt to control what materials decompose and where they decompose. In the process, you create a valuable soil amendment, reduce household waste, and start an avalanche of other personal and environmental benefits.

Backyard composting can involve a structure or some type of container, or you can integrate composting directly into your garden (described in Chapter 6). You can put as much or as little effort as you choose into your composting, depending on how quickly you want a finished product. The process of backyard composting is very forgiving, so even when you make mistakes, you end up with pretty darn good compost.

In nature, there is no waste—everything decomposes and continues in a circle to nourish new life. Nature takes decades and sometimes centuries to create beautiful, humus-filled topsoil (humus is the organic component of soil formed by decomposition). Trees release leaves that naturally decompose where they fall. Animals contribute manure, regularly adding a rich, nutrient-filled material to the cycle. Decomposers, such as earthworms, help break everything down and slowly build the topsoil year after year. When you compost in the backyard, you're replicating what happens naturally, but in a concentrated and controlled manner. You're creating that humus material you find on the forest floor. You're just not waiting hundreds of years to get it done.

Now that you have an idea of what backyard composting is, let's take a look at the benefits that compost offers your garden. Oh, how I love you, compost—let me count the ways . . . .

Composting in your backyard replicates what happens naturally on the forest floor.

> "My whole life has been spent waiting for an epiphany, a manifestation of God's presence, the kind of transcendent, magical experience that lets you see your place in the big picture. And that is what I had with my first compost heap."

—BETTE MIDLER, *LOS ANGELES TIMES*, MAY 8, 1996

Improving Your Soil

Whether you live in an area with soil so sandy that it holds no water, urban soil that needs some TLC, or heavy clay soil that only the toughest plant roots—or sharpest spade—can penetrate, compost can help. Experienced gardeners know the value of amending soil with compost. Backyard composting creates a rich, loamy material with beneficial microorganisms that bring life to your soil.

When we compost in our backyards, we condense the decomposition process happening naturally to create a rich, humus-filled material in a matter of a few months to a year. The end product makes plants stand up and cheer with excitement. They'd hug you if they could (or at least give you a high-five).

Mending Your Soil's Relationship with Water

Soil scientists explain that soil structure breaks down to three basic components: sand, silt, and clay. Sandy soils with large spaces between particles tend to drain too quickly. Heavy clay soils, on the other hand, have tiny spaces in between their very small particles and can retain too much water and drown your plants' roots.

Just as a natural humus layer would, compost helps improve the relationship that both sandy and clay soils have with water. The organisms that break down organic material release a sticky, glue-like substance that helps bind soil particles into a crumbly texture. The irregularly shaped clumps of compost-amended soil create spaces for air and act like a sponge to hold water. Compost aerates heavy clay soils by adding more spaces for air and providing the opportunity for water to drain when the soil becomes saturated.

In other words, compost gives your soil the sponge-like, water-retaining quality preferred by most plants. Adding just 5 percent more compost to your soil could quadruple your soil's capacity to hold water.

As if that wasn't enough, using compost as a mulch also improves the soil underneath. The compost layer acts like a barrier, protecting the underlying soil from losing moisture through evaporation. Plants in sunny or hot climates are especially grateful for this service; without a protective layer, their soil dries out soon after watering.

Soil 101

UNDERSTANDING the basics of soil science helps you better understand how compost can benefit your soil. Healthy soil naturally has layers (or horizons, if you want to get fancy) that develop over time. Each soil layer or horizon consists of different materials and textures. Obviously, soil in Arizona will differ from soil in Michigan, which will differ from soil in Florida. Diverse climates produce varied depths and makeups of soil layers.

In most temperate climates, soil will have the following basic soil layers. On top, a humus or litter layer (O Horizon) contains decaying plant and animal matter. The O Horizon teems with lots of soil bacteria, fungi, and other friendly soil life. This layer most closely resembles our finished compost, and the layer benefits greatly from the addition of compost.

The A Horizon, or topsoil layer, comes next. Rich in humus and mineral material, this layer is thicker than O Horizon and is also biologically active. Adding compost to this horizon will increase the humus material and improve the soil. Every gardener dreams of a nice thick layer of topsoil.

Below the A Horizon is the B Horizon, or subsoil layer. Although this layer has a low humus content, it is rich in minerals and offers a nice stable layer for deeper roots. While shoveling in your garden, you will sometimes reach this layer and notice a slowdown in your digging progress.

C Horizon is sometimes called the substratum or parent material. This layer consists of large, unbroken rocks and contains very little plant or animal life. Unless you dig very deep, you are unlikely to reach C Horizon. Bedrock lies beneath this layer.

Mimicking these natural soil layers will improve the soil in your garden for your plants. Adding soil to the top layers increases the microbial activity in the soil. These microbes will start mining the mineral nutrients in the lower levels, making them more available for your plants.

As a composter and, likely, a gardener, please understand that compost is not soil. It does not contain the vast number of minerals plants need to survive. The compost we create improves our soil and mimics the natural top layer of soil. We call it a "soil amendment" or a "soil conditioner" but never "soil" and certainly never the cringeworthy "dirt."

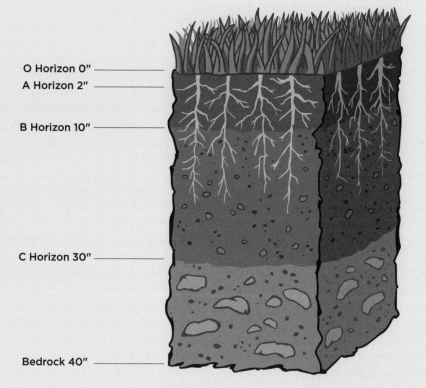

O Horizon 0"
A Horizon 2"
B Horizon 10"
C Horizon 30"
Bedrock 40"

Layers of soil contain different amounts of organic materials and minerals and serve different functions in nature. Mimicking these layers in your garden can benefit your plants.

> "Soil, he told us, isn't
> a substance to hold up plants
> in order that they may be
> fed with artificial fertilizers,
> and we who treated it as
> such were violating the cycle
> of nature. We must give back
> what we took away."

—ELEANOR PERÉNYI, *GREEN THOUGHTS*,
SPEAKING ABOUT J. I. RODALE

Adding Essential Nutrients to the Soil

Plants need 16 essential chemical elements for growth. The most prominent of these include hydrogen and oxygen (typically pulled from the air and water), carbon, nitrogen, phosphorus, and potassium. Of course, calcium, magnesium, sulfur, iron, manganese, and many others are also important. Compost helps your plants obtain these nutrients in two ways.

First, compost contains many of these nutrients because the material you added—leaves, food scraps, coffee grounds, and more—contained these nutrients. As the material breaks down in your compost, many of these nutrients become available for plant consumption.

Second, and arguably more important, compost improves the environment in your soil to encourage more microbial activity. The microorganisms in the soil make the nutrients available to your plants and can start pulling minerals from the surrounding soil to feed your plants. Compost improves the living area of the soil for the microorganisms so they grow, reproduce, and prosper.

On the more sciency side of the explanation, compost improves the soil's "cation exchange capacity."

This is what soil scientists use to measure the soil's capacity to hold on to essential nutrients and measure the soil's capacity to buffer against soil acidification (which is as bad as it sounds).

Compost is not fertilizer. People design fertilizer to feed plants. Compost feeds the soil. This distinction may seem minor to those who do not understand that soil is not a barren lifeless matter but a whole ecosystem teeming with life. The compost we add improves the life in the soil thereby helping to nourish the plants.

Increasing Soil Aeration

Amending your soil with compost improves the soil tilth. If you have heavy clay soils, the compost will break apart the tight structure, making the soil more friable for better aeration and drainage. Plant roots will have an easier time growing in the amended soil, and the varied structure of the compost will hold small pockets of air for both the roots and the organisms living in the soil. The gift that keeps on giving, compost also creates a soil habitat where macroinvertebrates thrive. Those little creatures moving around in the soil will continue to keep the soil aerated into the future.

Preventing Erosion

When raindrops hit bare soil, they have so much energy that they can blow apart particles on the surface of the soil. The wet soil particles then separate by size and density, creating layers as they settle, with the finest soil particles settling on top. This process forms a crust on the soil that prevents water from penetrating to the lower layers of soil (and your plants' roots). The newly formed crust also becomes prone to cracking where the streams of water form while running off. Soil cracking and crust creation begin the process of soil erosion and degradation. A nice layer of compost on the top of the soil cushions the falling raindrops, absorbing the energy and protecting the soil underneath.

The large amount of organic matter in compost also acts like a bonding agent in the soil structure. The compost will hold the soil in place against rain and wind. When you place compost on a sloped area, it will reduce the soil's natural inclination to slide down the hill. Engineers, farmers, and soil conservationists all recognize this benefit and will use compost on sites susceptible to soil erosion. You can also tap into this compost superpower and apply compost to areas where erosion may pull away your soil.

Suppressing Plant Disease

The type of organic material and microorganisms present in the soil could influence whether a plant gets sick or not. As you read this book, very smart people are researching why plants grown in compost have resistance to some plant diseases. Researchers try to optimize the composting process to increase the beneficial microorganisms acting as superheroes for your plants.

As backyard composters, we do not need to understand why compost seems to suppress plant disease. We can just smile knowing the compost we add to our soil could prevent our plants from getting sick.

Stabilizing pH

You have probably only considered the relative acidity or basicity of your soil if you have tried to add special plants to your garden, such as blueberries or azaleas. The pH of your soil influences what plants thrive and where. Some areas of the world have soils measuring more acidic, while others have soils measuring more basic. Compost helps stabilize the pH of your soil and usually brings it to neutral, the preferred state by most plants. Adding compost helps your soil resist a change in pH.

You Have the Power to Improve Your Soil

Amending your soil with compost is one of the most important actions you can take to improve and preserve soil in your garden. Soil conservationists would probably rank not tilling and planting cover crops toward the top of the list as well. If traditional farmers had easier access to large amounts of compost, you would see them using this miracle amendment more often. The good news is that we have the power to make compost in our own backyards. We generate raw compostable materials every day in our kitchens and gardens. Since we work on a smaller scale as individuals, the process of creating compost happens naturally and easily. We only need to seize the opportunity to create this amazing soil amendment.

Saving Money

Have you ever looked at the price of buying compost at a garden store? While I am not suggesting you start marketing your compost to your neighbors, backyard composting will save your family money in a variety of ways. Most obviously, you will not need to hand over half your paycheck to purchase bagged or bulk compost to improve your garden. Backyard compost is a free soil additive.

Since compost provides nutrients and creates a soil environment conducive to the microorganisms giving your plants nutrients, you will need to use less fertilizer to keep your garden vibrant.

Using compost in your garden also reduces the need to water your plants. Compost shades the soil and helps poor soils retain water. Fewer times turning on the hose equals more money in your pocket.

If you pay for trash by the bag, taking care of your yard trimmings and food scraps in your own backyard means a lower garbage bill. At the very least, it gives you something productive to do with those materials instead of setting them out on the curb.

Sharing Your Compost Love with Kids

Composting should be a basic life skill children learn along with growing their own food, cooking a basic meal, and sewing on a button. The best part of teaching children about composting is that they are so eager to learn. Ask any parent who does laundry—kids love dirt! Most children will develop an appreciation for the organisms in a compost pile if given a chance.

Compost piles contain a miniature food web and offer a great opportunity to observe nature. Open up the bin and dig around with the garden fork. What wildlife can your kids find? If you keep your cool with the creepy crawlies, so will the youngsters.

If you want a project to involve kids from the start, consider creating an indoor vermicomposting bin (composting with worms). Chapter 7 goes through the steps to create a DIY worm composting system and provides lots of fun facts about worms to share. Vermicomposting also allows you to give in to their pleas for a pet without adopting a 50-pound fur ball (no offense to dog lovers).

Involving kids in using the final product of finished compost helps them appreciate one of the primary benefits of compost. Use your harvested compost with children to pot flowers or herbs following the recipe in Chapter 8.

Creating and maintaining a worm composting bin is a great family project.

Part of a Zero-Waste Lifestyle

BEFORE you start rolling your eyes and say something about the impossibility of creating zero waste, hear me out. Most people think of zero waste as a long-term goal, something to strive toward in our efforts to reduce how much waste we create. Composting at home delivers one part of the plan that also incorporates refusing to buy or consume items that create waste, reducing unnecessary waste, reusing materials over and over, and of course, recycling everything possible.

Most people striving to create zero waste continually look at what trash they throw out and think of new ways to reduce or eliminate that garbage. They will bring their own bags to stores, use reusable containers when shopping and ordering takeout, and make some products at home (even toothpaste!). Everyone has to eat, so composting inedible food scraps becomes a major component of zero-waste living. Regardless of whether you choose to strive for zero waste or not, by composting at home, you do reduce your garbage, and that should make you feel a little warm and fuzzy.

Compost Makes You Happier

DON'T YOU LOVE when science proves something you have always known? Scientists have found a substance in soil and compost that acts as a natural antidepressant. *Mycobacterium vaccae* mirrors the effects of antidepressant drugs on neurons by stimulating serotonin production, making you relaxed and happy.

When you are working with compost or soil in the garden, you inhale these bacteria or come in contact with the bacteria through your skin. Contact with these bacteria causes a series of internal reactions triggering your body to release serotonin, a natural mood stabilizer. Scientists are currently researching how this may one day be used to treat depression, but in the meantime, we can use this as an excuse to go outside and play in the garden.

> ## "This heap of rotting vegetable matter looked more lovely to me than the tallest spike of the bluest delphinium."
>
> **—MICHAEL POLLAN,** *SECOND NATURE: A GARDENER'S EDUCATION*

Improving Your Health

Yes, composting, like gardening, will burn some calories and give you a reason to take at least a short walk every day. But compost also has an amazing effect on the food you grow in your backyard. Plants grown in nutrient-rich soil maximize their absorption of mineral nutrients that you need to survive. The more nutrients they absorb, the more we consume when we eat the fruit or vegetable. Your body will break down those nutrients using enzymes and take what it needs.

Plants grown in nutrient-deficient soil will not be able to absorb the maximum amount of nutrients that they would in nutrient-rich soils. Growing your own vegetables in your nutrient-rich, compost-amended soil could increase the number of important vitamins and minerals you consume.

Environmental Benefits

You may have heard the saying "think global, act local." Backyard composting embraces this philosophy. Setting aside materials from our trash to create a resource for your own backyard can positively affect the environment on a global scale. Sometimes it is hard to imagine that one little person or household can really make a difference to something as large as our planet, but imagine the impact if everyone on your block, your neighborhood, or your city started composting in their backyards. What we do matters.

Feeding Your Landscape, Not the Landfill

Depending on where you live and how much trash you throw away, compostable yard trimmings, food waste, and paper could make up between one-third and one-half of your garbage. In the United States, about 30 percent of the garbage a household creates could easily be composted in the backyard (about 1,234 pounds per year). This doesn't include the newspaper and cardboard that we could compost but generally recycle.

By composting the material in your backyard, your compostables do not take up space in the garbage truck. The truck will pick up more houses per trip, reducing the fuel needed to collect the route. Your materials also do not take up space at the landfill, extending the life of that landfill and delaying the need to build more. Composting means you put less waste at the curb, leading to lighter garbage and yard waste trucks, longer life at the landfill, and smiles all around.

Reducing Your Carbon Footprint

Backyard composting reduces your carbon footprint, or the amount of greenhouse gases that living your life generates. When plants decompose, they naturally release the carbon dioxide (CO_2) absorbed during their lives. Plants and food scraps also do this in your compost bin. It's okay; that's what they're supposed to do.

But when buried in the landfill with no air, food and yard waste decompose anaerobically and release methane instead. Methane traps heat in our atmosphere and has an impact 25 times greater than CO_2 over a 100-year period. In other words, by encouraging the right kind of decomposition, you reduce the greenhouse-gas impact of your yard trimmings and food scraps and lessen global climate change. Yay for you!

Restoring life to our soil through compost also allows soil to amazingly store carbon so that it never becomes CO_2 in our atmosphere. This magic trick starts with plants growing in your fertile soil. Plants pull CO_2 out of the air in the process we all know and love: photosynthesis. What the plant doesn't use during photosynthesis is pulled down to the roots and given to the organisms in the soil surrounding the roots. Those soil organisms, especially the fungi, use and stabilize the carbon in a form that the soil can store for thousands of years. A trick like that deserves a standing ovation.

Curbside Residential Organics Collection

SEPARATE collection of curbside yard trimmings for composting is fairly mainstream in the United States, Canada, and Europe. However, more and more communities have begun offering curbside collection of food scraps. Sometimes communities allow residents to commingle food scraps with yard trimmings and compost all the materials together. Other times, especially in urban areas with few yard trimmings, the collection involves placing food scraps in a container separate from trash and recycling.

Even for backyard composters, these collections have benefits. Most notably, curbside collection of organics means that the material goes to a large industrial-level composting operation that usually takes all food scraps, including meats and cheeses. These operations also have large grinders and chippers to handle branches and trees that are impossible to compost with most backyard methods. Large-scale professional composting operations use technologies that can handle the potentially stinky or bulky materials we do not want in our backyard bins. Even if you compost in your backyard, you can send your fish heads, chicken bones, and large tree branches to be handled by the professionals.

As much as we want to spread the compost love, some neighbors will never adopt backyard composting. Curbside collections allow these neighbors to give their compostables a new life.

This smaller-scale, four-corral composting area serves a community garden across from an elementary school and is the perfect size for children helpers. Students come to the garden to learn about gardening and composting and share in the harvest.

Small-Scale Community Composting

A GROWING movement across the United States, Canada, and Europe pulls together people living in a community to share a common composting area. These sites most often occur in community gardens, in schools, or even on small farms. Composting on a small scale, using locally based resources, allows residents who may not have backyards or the means to compost in their backyards access to composting. This decentralized form of composting also keeps organic resources in the community since the community garden or other host site often uses the finished compost on the property.

Aside from all the usual benefits of composting, neighbors getting together to compost as a community has additional advantages. Household-scale backyard composting tends to be a very private affair. We go about our business of collecting materials, maintaining the compost pile, and using the compost in a solitary or family-oriented manner. Community composting brings neighbors together and raises awareness for neighbors who have not yet been exposed to the wonderful world of composting. Gathering with your neighbors to create a valuable soil amendment using your collective labor and resources is a powerful feeling.

Community-scaled composting can occasionally go awry, especially when the system lacks a competent manager. If you are venturing into community-scaled composting, consider these tips:

1 Dedicate a manager who knows how to compost. This person could be someone experienced in composting in their own backyard or someone who has taken formal classes on backyard composting. This person should train everyone else involved in the maintenance of the site.

2 Consider what scale of composting site you need. Many community composting sites operate just over the size of a typical backyard system. How many people will be contributing materials?

3 Research local regulations. Some states and municipalities have regulations restricting the size of the compost area or what types of materials you can add. Look into your local regulations and operate accordingly. If regulations are too strict, consider requesting a variance for your site. It never hurts to ask.

4 Choose a system that can handle your volume. For some community composting sites, this means having multiple types of compost bins. Others construct large two- or three-bin units. If space allows, some community compost sites operate large compost piles called "windrows."

5 Consider your area and whether having a locking lid or other critter-proof mechanisms are necessary. Nothing spurs neighbors to complain like a haven for unwanted pests.

6 Educate participants on what to compost. If you allow neighbors to bring food scraps, make sure they know only to bring fruit and vegetable scraps and to leave out meat and dairy. Limiting the types of materials will make the manager's life easier. Do not allow compostable plastics or any other hard-to-handle material such as prepared cooked foods. Create clear signage at the site to show where participants should place material and how the compost system works.

7 Consider the final product. Will the community garden, school, or farm use the finished compost on site? Will you allow participants to take some of the finished compost? This is also a reason to consult local regulations. Sometimes regulations do not allow you to move the material off site or sell the material. It's better to be safe than sorry.

Community-scaled composting offers a great opportunity to build community, replenish local soils, and provide access to small-scale composting for your neighbors. While the process of designing and implementing this level of composting is more tedious than composting in your own backyard, you may find that the benefits of dividing compost-related labor with your neighbors will outweigh the initial concerns. You may also get to know those living around you and make some new friends.

Cleaning Polluted Soil

We know compost has amazing superpowers, but this one is truly impressive: compost binds heavy metals, polycyclic aromatic hydrocarbons (PAHs), and other nasty toxins in the soil to prevent them from migrating into the water or being absorbed by plants. If you have urban soil with a sketchy past, compost could help improve your soil. Compost microbes are even able to degrade some toxic organic compounds such as petroleum (hydrocarbons). On a larger scale than your backyard, companies use compost to bioremediate soils contaminated with petroleum.

Preventing Pollutants in Storm Water

When it rains, water washes over all the exposed surfaces—driveways, parking lots, farm fields—and picks up and washes away chemicals or materials on those surfaces. So, if you recently salted your driveway or if the farmer recently fertilized his field, rain will pick that up and carry it away. We call this "storm water runoff" (or nonpoint source pollution). This water and all its hitchhikers end up in streams, rivers, and eventually the ocean. As you might imagine, extra salt, fertilizers, and chemical pollutants can cause issues in these aquatic habitats, hurting fish, coral, and all the other creatures that call these wet wonderlands their home.

Because compost can bind heavy metals and other contaminants, it acts as a filter for storm water and has been shown to minimize leaching of pesticides and other chemicals in soil systems. We may not have power over what a farmer sprays on his field or what a neighbor's leaky truck spills on the road, but we can control what happens in our backyard. Any water passing through compost will end up a little cleaner.

Replenishing Depleted World Soil

Another larger environmental issue we hear little about is the striking amount of soil depleted every year in the world. According to the Food and Agriculture Organization of the United Nations, about one-third of the world's soils have already experience degradation from chemical-heavy farming techniques, deforestation, and global climate change. Given the importance of soil in growing one of the primary staples of our lives— food—this issue deserves at least a nod.

While alarming, I do not mean to distress you with this rather depressing issue. Smart and passionate people develop and implement solutions to this problem every day. Of course, one of the best solutions is applying— you guessed it—compost. As we have already discussed, compost amends the soil, improving nutrient availability, decreasing erosion, and improving soil structure. Just know you are doing your part to impact this global issue by composting in your own backyard.

You Can Do It!

After listing more benefits than you probably ever imagined could possibly come from your old banana peel, let me leave you with one last slightly intangible benefit: backyard composting is self-empowering. This benefit goes beyond helping the environment, saving money, and improving your garden, which are all benefits with value; each alone could be enough to persuade you to compost. You must experience the empowering feeling to truly understand.

In our consumer-driven society, backyard composting gives us an outlet for creation and regeneration. From the pile of decaying rotten material, once useful and alive, we give death a new purpose. We create a valuable soil amendment with "waste" and our own blood, sweat, and tears (though with any luck, not too much blood or tears).

Intentionally, we gather the potato peels, dry crispy leaves, and dead plants from last year's garden. We invite a few billion micro- and macroorganisms and tend to the pile as we would a garden, giving it water, feeding it with food scraps, and incorporating air. Backyard composting rewards our attention by providing us the most powerful soil amendment available, ready to transform our tired, spent soil with fresh life and humus. As my fellow compost enthusiast Brad Miller says, composting allows you to give birth to new soil. The compost we create improves our backyard soil, over time transforming the landscape from one reliant on artificial fertilizers to an independent, nearly self-sustaining system.

People drawn to backyard composting for the environmental or gardening benefits often continue because of the personal satisfaction that comes from harvesting and using finished compost. I imagine you would get the same feeling from building your own furniture or making your own bread from scratch. It is the satisfactory accomplishment of creating something on your own with no help. After you harvest your compost, you can sit back to admire your creation. You made it, and you should be proud.

Take Action to Prevent Wasted Food

SETTING aside food scraps for composting in your backyard makes you keenly aware of how much food you waste. Some things, such as banana peels and melon rinds, are unavoidable. Others, such as the slimy zucchini forgotten in the back of the produce drawer and the moldy strawberries we meant to eat, could have been avoided. Bringing the inedible food that had so much potential back to the compost pile for a productive burial doesn't seem like enough.

Everything we eat tells a story, from the labor of the farmer, the soil and water used to grow the food, the fuel to transport the food, and the energy to keep the food fresh in the store and your home. Everything we eat requires so many resources. Composting what we waste is certainly better than just sending it to the landfill, but we can take a few steps to reduce wasted food in our households (and save money at the same time):

1 Grocery shop with intention. Take stock of what you have in your pantry and refrigerator and plan your meals ahead to use up foods before they go bad. Create a grocery list and stick to the list as best you can.

2 Make use of your freezer. This impressive appliance helps you hit pause and preserve your food to eat another day. You can freeze most foods in some way or another. Prepared foods such as soups and casseroles make great meals when you don't feel like cooking. Peel bananas past their prime and freeze them for later use in sweet, delicious smoothies.

3 Revive your food. Bendy carrots and wilted lettuce will crisp up if you place them in an ice-water bath for 5 to 10 minutes. Stale bread and crackers become tastier when toasted in the oven for a few minutes. Transform overcooked veggies into a sauce or soup with a blender.

Perhaps the best way to reduce wasted food and take advantage of composting is to create a broth bag in your freezer. When a recipe calls for half an onion and you know you won't be able to use the other half, place the other half in the freezer bag. When you only need the caps of those portobello mushrooms, place the stems in the freezer bag. After slicing the kale leaves off the center rib, toss the ribs and stems into the bag. You can put almost any unused vegetable in this bag. Once you fill the bag, create a stock by simmering the vegetables in water for 30 minutes or until they are well-cooked. Strain off the liquid and use the broth to make a soup or freeze it for later. Then scoop up all those mushy vegetables and bring them to your compost pile. They will decompose with dignity, knowing you squeezed every penny out of that produce.

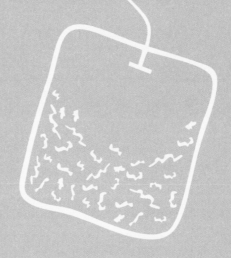

2

THE SCIENCE OF COMPOSTING

THE SECRET GOAL
OF COMPOSTING

If maintained correctly, your backyard compost bin contains an entire food web with billions of organisms working together to decompose your food scraps into rich, beautiful compost. You do not need to have an extensive knowledge of the science behind composting to compost well, but this is a fascinating world. Come, geek out with me, and let's throw a little party to learn how composting works.

Earthworms are a composter's best friend.

First, I'll let you in on a little secret. Everything we do when composting, from constructing the bin to maintaining the pile, is all to keep the micro- and macroorganisms in your bin alive and happy. If you properly maintain your compost, the environment you create becomes the ideal habitat for creatures you can see and creatures you cannot see. These organisms work together, transforming your banana peels into beautiful, crumbly compost. To have a successful compost party, we need to supply our little friends with the right amount of air, water, and food, but the service they provide is well worth our efforts. Learning more about the guests at your composting party will help you better appreciate everything they do to make your composting process a success.

Macroorganisms: Creatures You Can See

Although they are not the most numerous or even the most important organisms in your compost, macroorganisms such as worms, centipedes, millipedes, and beetles have a role to play in our controlled decomposition. Since these are the creatures you will

most likely see, we will go through a few examples from each group.

Our favorite macroorganisms, the decomposers, eat bacteria, fungi, rotting vegetables, and leaves. These include worms, millipedes, sowbugs, and springtails. The larvae from beetles and most other creatures also fall in this group. These organisms help break down particles in the pile and contribute manure.

Worms and other macro decomposers are the friends who show up before the party really starts to get things ready and then stay well after it is over to help clean up, although when the party reaches its peak (the hottest stage of composting), you may find them off in the hallway conversing with your dog. The temperature in a very hot compost pile overwhelms most macroinvertebrates, so they tend to shy away until the heat subsides.

- **Millipedes:** These look like dark-colored worms with hard shells and many, many legs (two pairs for every segment). Millipedes have so many legs they remind me of a living toothbrush scurrying across your pile. Unlike their centipede cousins, millipedes feed mostly on plants and help break down material, but they will occasionally eat an insect carcass in their path. In the compost bin, millipedes typically grow 1 to 2 inches in size.

- **Sowbugs:** Think tiny armadillos and you will have an idea of what these segmented, fat-bodied crustaceans look like. Sowbugs eat decaying vegetation, so they tend to thrive in a compost pile. Delicate, platelike gills on their abdomen must be kept moist for these little guys to breath. Females lay many eggs at one time, so your pile can suddenly seem populated with sowbugs overnight. The eggs hatch into miniature versions of adults.

- **Springtails:** Although they're very small, you will recognize these wingless insects by their erratic jumping when you disturb the compost pile. Small, springlike structures under their abdomen catapult them into the air when they sense danger. In addition to eating decaying plants, these white or blue-gray jumpers also eat nematodes (small worms) and fungi.

- **Earthworms:** The heavyweight champions of the composting food web, earthworms consume an inspiring amount of material, turning and aerating the pile in the process. Their tunnels allow air, water, and other organisms deeper access to the pile. Mostly one long digestive system, earthworms grind food in their gizzards and use digestive juices to further break the material down. Their casts—worm poop—come out of the worm richer in bacteria, organic matter, and available nitrogen than what went into the worm. Earthworms provide both physical and chemical degradation of compostables. Of course, composters love earthworms, and I like to think they return the sentiment.

- **Snails and slugs:** Occasionally, these slimy friends make a brief appearance at our composting party. They mostly eat living plants, so they will eat only the freshest material in your compost heap, such as new plant trimmings and fresh food scraps. They mainly hang out at the edges, sometimes even climbing the walls of the bin. I sometimes feel like snails accidently show up, eat a little, and then move on to greener pastures (literally).

- **Mites:** If you know what to look for, you will see these very tiny critters quite often. Many different varieties hang out in compost piles, some you can see and some almost microscopic. They have eight leglike appendages and remind me of very tiny ticks—but only in appearance. Some varieties help with decomposition by eating the organic materials you toss in your pile, while others eat fungi and still others fall into our next category as predators. You will often see them hitching rides on the backs of other composting macroinvertebrates such as millipedes or beetles.

Other macroorganisms, the predatory variety, we tolerate at our composting party because they are part of a healthy food web. But when it comes to the real work of composting, their contribution is minimal. Hanging out at the top of the compost bin food chain, these creatures eat other animals in your compost (the ones actually working), but they do contribute their share of manure to the pile. Of course, some of the same creatures that are considered food for the predators will happily eat the predator's remains after they die.

Centipedes, pseudoscorpians, and predatory beetles fall into this group. These tolerated predators are like the people who show up to your party uninvited or your friend Lisa's annoying husband who eats all the guacamole. Luckily, a good party can only sustain a few of these "friends" and Lisa is the only one who has to go home with him.

- **Centipedes:** Segmented and wormlike, centipedes have a pair of legs on each segment and slowly grow into adults after hatching from eggs laid during the warm months. If you spy one, it will likely be scurrying fast in the top few inches of your pile. With formidable claws located behind their head, centipedes can inject poison to paralyze their prey. You can tell the difference between centipedes and their more docile cousins, the millipedes, because centipedes have very defined legs and a flattened body while millipedes have almost toothbrush-looking legs and a rounded body shape.

- **Pseudoscorpions:** Although they have a pretty scary name, the largest pseudoscorpions are about the size of a grain of rice. They seize victims with their front claws and then inject venom from the tips of their claws to immobilize their prey. Pseudoscorpions eat mites, larvae, and small earthworms.

- **Rove and ground beetles:** You can easily spot beetles with their two pairs of wings and because of their larger size. Although many other types of beetles will eat plants, rove and ground beetles soar over the pile like falcons, capturing and devouring snails, worms, and other creatures in the bin. Compost bins are ideal places for beetles to lay their eggs so that the hatching larvae (maggots) can feast on the rotting material.

When backyard composting, you do not need to add earthworms (or any other organism) to your pile. If you build it, they will come. Earthworms and other macroorganisms will naturally squirm, crawl, or hop into your pile and accept decaying matter as payment for their invaluable service.

Other macroorganisms you will see in your compost include flies, spiders, and many others. A thriving population of macroorganisms in your compost pile should be a point of pride, not a matter of concern.

Microorganisms and Fungi

In order for the inhabitants of your compost bin to turn food scraps and dry leaves into rich, luscious compost, you need both physical degradation of the material into smaller pieces and chemical transformation of the material. Bacteria, actinomycetes, protozoa, and fungi perform the necessary chemical decomposition services. While all these organisms play their part, bacteria perform the lion's share of the work.

- **Bacteria:** The type of bacteria in your compost bin will vary depending on where you live, what material you put in, the time of year, and how often you turn your pile. But regardless of what you do or do not do, bacteria are there. Bacteria coat every surface of everything in your pile. This is good news for composters because bacteria are among the most adaptable eaters on the planet, able to produce the needed enzymes to digest just about anything you put in front of them.

Bacteria represent the bulk of your friends. They are always at the party. They are active in every conversation, they heat up the party with the pumping bass, and they eat almost any snack you offer, from the carrot sticks to the chicken wings. (Disclaimer: All this party talk is just an analogy. Do not add chicken wings to your real compost pile. The pumping bass is optional.)

These microorganisms operate under the "live hard, die young" philosophy, usually only having a lifespan of 20 to 30 minutes. But one single-celled organism can yield a progeny of billions in just a few hours. You may remember from school that a piece of garden soil the size of a pea can contain a billion bacteria.

- **Fungi:** Most types of fungi living in your compost bin are saprophytes, organisms that obtain energy by breaking down organic matter in dead or dying plants and animals—just the kind of decomposer we want to invite to the party. Although you will occasionally see some fuzzy mold on items kept in your kitchen collector too long, fungi do tend to show up late to the compost-making party. Most of their work begins after the pile has heated and cooled in the final stages of composting.

Plasmodial Slime Mold

PLASMODIAL slime mold not only sounds like a creature from a science fiction movie (*The Blob*, anyone?), but it also *looks* like a creature from a science fiction movie. Sometimes bright green, yellow, or hot pink, plasmodial slime mold needs wet, warm conditions to survive and is actually very rare to encounter. This gelatinous mass is a type of protist or microscopic animal that feeds on bacteria growing in mulch.

Should you encounter plasmodial slime mold in your compost bin, do not panic. It will likely dry out and go away quickly and is not harmful to your compost. I do recommend taking a few photos so your friends believe that you were visited by a strange alien species.

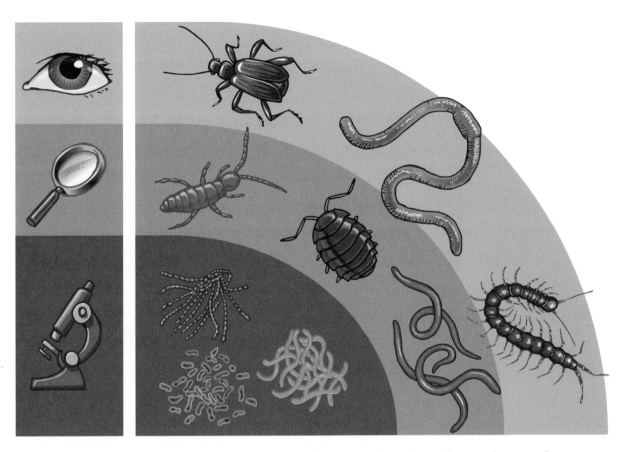

Macro- and microorganisms in your compost pile include many different types of organisms working together to transform your scraps and trimmings into finished compost.

Fungi include molds (moulds) and yeasts, and most of time, you will not even see they are present. They work as unseen filaments breaking down tough debris the bacteria cannot handle. Occasionally, you will spot a cute pop-up mushroom or find white fuzzy mold covering the moist surface of the pile, but these are all good signs that fungi continue doing their job.

- **Actinomycetes:** "You smell like actinomycetes" is probably the highest compliment you could bestow on a composter. These organisms are the "earthy" in an earthy scent and give finished compost and freshly plowed earth their signature smell. Similar to fungi but also bacteria, these creatures are critical to making compost. If you see something that looks like spider webs stretching through the first few inches of your pile, you have found colonies of actinomycetes growing in long, threadlike filaments.

Actinomycetes have special enzymes allowing them to break down woody stems and bark. Although some species of this group show up when your pile heats up, like fungi does, they tend to arrive toward the end of the compost party. They are doing your dishes and packing away leftover food alongside your macroinvertebrate friends.

- **Nematodes:** If you look under a magnifying lens, nematodes look like very fine human hairs but are actually cylindrical microscopic worms. Although microscopic, they are the most abundant physical decomposer in a compost pile. They do not chemically transform compost like bacteria and fungi do. Nematodes eat decaying matter much like an earthworm; they just do it on a much smaller scale. These transparent worms are so small that 90,000 nematodes can dine on one rotting apple.

We Are All in This Together

As a composter, your job is to provide a habitat for these organisms to do their job of decomposition. Your food scraps and brown leaves add fuel to the system. The physical decomposers, such as the worms and the millipedes, grind their way through what you add, occasionally acting as dinner for someone higher up on the food chain, such as a centipede. The smallest organisms in the pile step in at different stages of decomposition to ultimately transform that apple core into our desired end product.

We provide water for these organisms to survive and air for them to breathe. We protect them from the strongest elements of weather to keep them working around the clock and most of the year. We supply a well-balanced diet of carbon and nitrogen to give our friends the nutrients they need to grow. If we succeed in providing the habitat, the macro- and microorganisms will succeed in making finished compost. After we harvest our brown gold, patting your tiny composting friends on the back is optional.

Mother Nature's Influence

The environment around your compost bin will also offer assistance in the natural breakdown of your materials. Rainwater will infiltrate your bin, helping keep the moisture content up. Sunlight will warm the pile and assist in maintaining the thermophilic stage. Freeze and thaw cycles will break apart the structure of materials and aid bacterial decomposition. Of course, Mother Nature has a fickle temperament and can also cause the destruction of the habitat you have created with too much rain, too much cold, or too much heat. Our job is to work with nature when we can and protect against nature when necessary to maintain the perfect habitat for our little decomposers.

Aerobic Versus Anaerobic

Not all decomposition is equal, and what happens in your compost pile will either fall into the anaerobic or the aerobic category. If we water our compost too much or do not provide enough air, we can create an environment where only the anaerobic bacteria want to live. For most types of backyard composting, the anaerobic bacteria are the bad guys (no offense to the little buggers; they just do what comes naturally). Anaerobic decomposition is like the most awkward work party you have ever attended, where time seems to move backward and you have to spend the whole evening in a boring conversation with smelly Simon. It is still a party, and anaerobic decomposition will eventually create compost, but, wow, there are much better ways to spend an evening.

Anaerobic bacteria break down material s-l-o-w-l-y and create smelly gases that will make even the stoutest of composters lose their lunch. Another word for anaerobic decomposition is *putrefaction*. Swamps owe their distinctive odors to anaerobic bacteria, and aside from a few specialized forms of composting, we do not want to replicate this slow, slimy, smelly decomposition in our backyards.

As if you needed more reason to dislike anaerobic decomposition in backyard composting, this type of decomposition releases mostly methane gas instead of the CO_2 released during aerobic decomposition. Methane absorbs more energy in our atmosphere than does carbon dioxide, resulting in a global warming potential 25 times higher than carbon dioxide.

Aerobic, or air-loving, bacteria are the good guys. They decompose material quickly and with little to no odor. We want to do everything we can to invite them in and have them stay a while. Different types of aerobic bacteria populate your compost during the three distinct phases of decomposition.

Stages of Decomposition

Your compost will go through a mesophilic, a thermophilic, and a maturation phase of decomposition if decomposing aerobically. Different organisms accompany each phase; some prefer the mild temperatures of the beginning and ending of the compost pile, while some like it hot.

THE THREE PHASES OF AEROBIC COMPOSTING

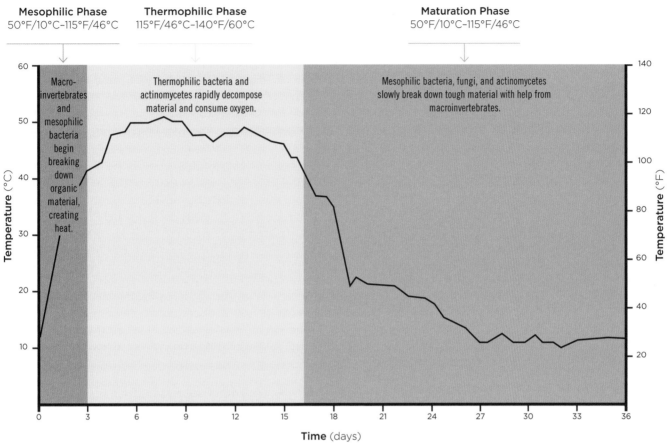

Mesophilic Phase
50°F/10°C–115°F/46°C

Thermophilic Phase
115°F/46°C–140°F/60°C

Maturation Phase
50°F/10°C–115°F/46°C

Macro-invertebrates and mesophilic bacteria begin breaking down organic material, creating heat.

Thermophilic bacteria and actinomycetes rapidly decompose material and consume oxygen.

Mesophilic bacteria, fungi, and actinomycetes slowly break down tough material with help from macroinvertebrates.

Temperature (°C)

Temperature (°F)

Time (days)

Materials decomposing in a compost pile go through three major stages marked by temperature, level of decomposition, and macro- and microorganisms present.

Mesophilic Phase

During the first phase, the mesophilic (moderate-temperature-loving) organisms start off the party. If you continually add material to your bin, everything you throw in for the first few days is in this stage. Colonies of bacteria travel to the party on the food scraps or dry leaves and start expanding under the right conditions. Macroorganisms such as larvae and worms also munch away on the delicious buffet you prepared. Mesophilic organisms generally prefer temperatures from 50 to 115°F. This stage of our composting party can last a few days to a few weeks, depending on the maturity of your pile, the balance of materials, and your climate.

The rapidly increasing numbers of mesophilic bacteria and fungi feast on the soluble sugars and starches of the material you added. In our party analogy, your growing number of friends start eating all the best cookies, cupcakes, and soft pretzels, but that's okay because everyone is having a good time. By eating all this food and breaking down the organic material in the pile, the mesophilic bacteria create heat as a byproduct.

Thermophilic Phase

Like most good parties, the composting process will eventually start to heat up. Once enough heat has built up from the action of the mesophilic bacteria, the thermophilic (heat-loving) organisms step in and thrive in these conditions. Thermophilic organisms prefer temperatures of roughly 115 to 140°F. Although predominantly bacteria, thermophiles also include heat-tolerant species of actinomycetes and fungi.

During this phase, the worms and other mesophilic organisms migrate to the edges of the pile or back into the cool earth. The specialized thermophilic bacteria decompose material rapidly and consume oxygen rapidly in the process. If you wish to maintain the high temperatures to keep your thermophilic friends quickly decomposing, you have to aerate the pile regularly during this time. Turning the pile during this phase also integrates new material previously not in the thermophilic zone, giving the thermophiles fresh food. If your compost pile is not large enough, too much heat will be lost to the outside air, and you will not achieve the temperatures needed for this phase.

The thermophilic phase lasts a few weeks to a few months, depending on what material you add and how often you turn the pile. The high temperatures of this phase kill pathogens and weed seeds. Organisms consume the proteins, fats, and cellulose in the pile. Cellulose is the major structural compound in plants, so this is the phase when the materials break apart and no longer resemble their original structures. However long it takes, eventually our heat-loving friends get tired and leave the party, bringing us to the calmer and final stage of composting.

Maturation Phase

This phase ushers in more mesophilic organisms for the long, slow finalization of our party. The food not yet consumed, such as lignin (the tough structures that make up wood and bark), is broken down by the fungi and actinomycetes. Worms jump in too and help clean up the material into a state of finished compost. This stage can last a few months, depending on the composition of your pile and the type of compost bin you use.

Although the compost in this phase measures close to air temperature, your microorganism and macroorganism friends are stabilizing the material and making the nutrients ready for plant use. When implementing some types of composting, such as using a tumbler, expect that the compost you harvest will complete this phase after you place it on the ground.

Compost Chemistry

Although it may seem like magic, our food scraps require no wand or fairy dust to become finished compost. Instead, they only need the "magic" of chemistry. Microorganisms fundamentally change the chemical makeup of the materials they eat, pulling off the energy they need using different enzymes. Bacteria and fungi secrete these enzymes to break down the complex compounds making up what we add to the compost bin. Impressively, they create specialized enzymes specifically for the type of material they are breaking down. For example, they secrete protease to digest proteins, cellulase to digest cellulose, and amylase to digest starches.

As the food moves through the composting food web, compounds change and simplify until most are simple and stable enough for plant intake. Some microbes, however, create long, intricate chains called polymers using the simpler compounds. Materials such as the lignin fibers in wood are so complex that the backyard composting process does not fully break it down. The simple compounds, complex compounds, and leftover lignin fibers mix together to become the beautiful humus-filled material we call finished compost.

Zen and the Art of Carbon and Nitrogen Balance

Our composting friends rely on you to provide fuel by adding your food scraps, dry leaves, and other materials to your pile. Every time these microorganisms multiply, they need building blocks to create new cells. Although this process requires many elements, the stars of the show are carbon and nitrogen. If you balance these two elements well, your microorganisms will have everything they need to rapidly reproduce and invite more friends to continue the decomposition party.

Microbes use carbon as an energy source and a building block for about 50 percent of their cells by weight. Luckily for us and our little decomposers, carbon is abundant in nature, as this element acts as the basis of all life on our planet. Everything you add to your compost will have at least some carbon. During the process of aerobic decomposition, microorganisms respire about two-thirds of the carbon as carbon dioxide (CO_2) and use the remaining carbon to combine with nitrogen in living cells. Put another way, our microscopic friends require a lot of carbon to do their job.

Nitrogen steps in as a key component of the proteins and enzymes the bacteria need when building their bodies and breaking down their food. When we discuss the carbon-nitrogen balance later in the book (see page 49), we will go into detail explaining what materials contain high levels of carbon and what materials contain high levels of nitrogen. To encourage optimal growth of our microorganism buddies, we need to supply the perfect amounts of carbon and nitrogen. Too much carbon and decomposition moves very slowly because microorganisms cannot find the nitrogen they need to build proteins and enzymes. Too much nitrogen will allow rapid microbial growth, but at some point, excess nitrogen creates ammonia gas, which smells awful, like very strong urine. In our party analogy, adding too much nitrogen would be like having too much alcohol at your party. Things might seem fun for a while, but you will be paying for it the next morning.

Aside from carbon and nitrogen, microorganisms require a number of other compounds to reproduce and break down your material into compost. Phosphorus, potassium, and hydrogen also contribute to the creation of cells or enzymes. Composters focus on carbon and nitrogen rather than these other elements since carbon and nitrogen tend to act as the main limiting factors in decomposition.

If you really want to geek out over composting science or you just love numbers, check out the table showing the carbon-to-nitrogen ratio of common compostable materials. In simple terms, we strive for three parts brown material (carbon rich) to every one part green material (nitrogen rich) to reach that magic balance. In scientific terms, the carbon-to-nitrogen ratios prove much more complicated. Rather than the 3:1 guideline of browns to greens we discuss in more detail later in the book, most compost scientists strive for a 30:1 ratio of carbon to

CARBON-TO-NITROGEN RATIO OF COMMON COMPOSTABLES

	Compostable Material	Carbon-to-Nitrogen Ratio
High in Carbon (Brown)	Brown leaves	30–80:1
	Straw	40–100:1
	Wood chips and sawdust	100–500:1
	Bark	100–130:1
	Mixed paper	150–200:1
	Newspaper or corrugated cardboard	560:1
	Pine needles	60–110:1
High in Nitrogen (Green)	Vegetable scraps	12–20:1
	Coffee grounds	20:1
	Grass clippings	12–25:1
	Cow and horse manure	20–25:1
	Chicken manure	10:1

Source: Composting to Reduce the Waste Stream: A Guide to Small Scale Food and Yard Waste Composting.

nitrogen (with some level of disagreement on whether 30:1 is, in fact, the ideal ratio).

Everything you add will have some carbon and a little nitrogen. If you add something with a relatively lower carbon-to-nitrogen ratio (meaning it's nitrogen rich) to your compost, such as coffee grounds, you have to balance it with a material relatively higher in carbon, such as brown leaves. Compost scientists will use these known ratios to calculate the precise mix to add and create perfect compost. We, on the other hand, are just having a compost party. Do not worry about digging out the calculator every time you go to your compost bin. I include this table of ratio numbers not to overcomplicate composting, but so that you can appreciate the interesting and diverse makeup of different materials.

The Yin and Yang of Oxygen and Water

All the guests at our composting party need air to breathe and water to survive. Too much of one cancels out the other, however, so a successful composter maintains a pile moist enough to provide our microbe friends enough water to survive but not so much that the pile has no oxygen. If the pile is about as wet as a wrung-out sponge, a film of water will coat each particle in the bin but have pockets of air surrounding the particle. This thin film of water on the surface of particles is where most of the microbe activity happens. Like the kitchen of your house, this is where everyone wants to be during your party.

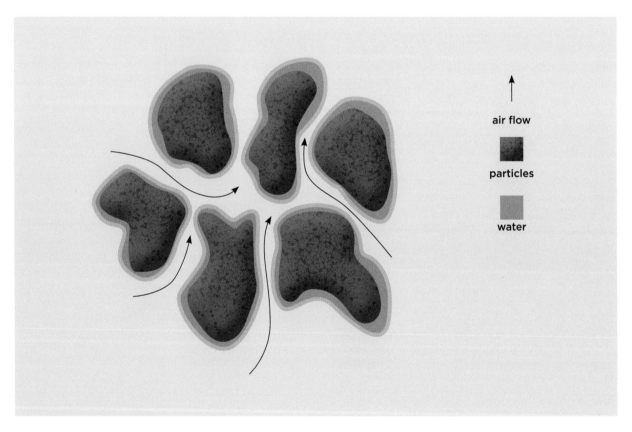

air flow

particles

water

Maintaining the perfect amount of moisture in your compost pile will coat each particle with water and allow air to move through the materials.

Aside from water, particle size is another factor affecting the air flow through your pile. We go into detail later in the book on the best size or mix of sizes of material (see page 50), but imagine the difference in the size of sawdust and wood chips. Obviously, wood chips will have vastly more air space between the particles than the sawdust. However, the sawdust offers easier eating (more available carbon) to our microbe friends. As they decompose the sawdust particles, microorganisms will quickly consume the air in between the tiny particles, effectively ending their feast prematurely. Balancing the need for air and your microbe friends' desire for fast food will give you the fastest composting results.

Unless you live in a very arid environment, food scraps and rainwater supply your compost pile with all the water it needs for most of the year. Fresh food scraps have a moisture content of 70 to 90 percent water by weight. Many fresh yard trimmings also contain a high percentage of water. As your composting friends break down the structure of the food and other materials, they release water into the compost pile. Only with very dry weather will the pile require you to add more water.

Optimum pH for Your Compost

In case you missed that week in science class, pH represents the relative acidity or basicity of a water-containing solution. The scale generally runs from 1 to 14, although extremes exist outside of those boundaries. Pure water is neither acidic nor basic but neutral at 7.0. Anything below that is acidic, and anything above is basic. Most bacteria can tolerate a pH range between 6.0 and 7.5, whereas fungi tolerate a wider pH range between 5.5 and 8.0. If the pile becomes too acidic or too basic, most of your micro- and macroorganism friends will pack up and leave.

What you add to your compost can affect the acidity of the habitat. Too much citrus could lower the pH to an intolerable acidity. Too much wood ash could raise the pH beyond 7.5, essentially killing off your bacteria. Unless you are adding a very large amount of citrus or wood ash, the bulk of the pile will neutralize these acidic and basic materials. Feel free to add all

the citrus peels associated with your normal daily life, but should you start a fresh-squeezed lemonade stand, resulting in a 5-gallon bucket full of squeezed lemons, add the material sparingly to your compost.

Compost Happens

Obviously, decomposition happens in nature and is an essential part of the nutrient cycle to transform the finite matter on this planet from death to life and back again. As composters, we attempt, usually successfully, to somewhat control this process in our backyards by creating the best habitat for our favorite decomposers and combining old leaves and leftover food scraps in the hopes of producing something wonderful.

I find that remembering the "little people" who do the actual work in the compost pile (the bacteria, fungi, earthworms, etc.) helps me maintain a successful composting system. Like guests at a party, I want to make sure they are happy and have everything they need. When I dig into my compost, I can imagine billions upon billions of bacteria quietly munching away, and I want to do what I can to support their efforts. In perspective, our work as composters pales in comparison to what all our micro and macro friends contribute. Thanks, little buddies—we appreciate that you make our compost party possible!

3

COMPOSTING BASICS

WHAT CAN I COMPOST?

At its most basic, what you can compost in your backyard boils down to this question: did it come from a plant? If the answer is yes, then most likely you can compost it in your backyard. As with all things, there are exceptions to this rule. Some materials take longer to decompose than others, and some materials, such as food scraps, require special treatment. You will find that different methods of composting handle special materials with varying levels of success.

Rake up that bountiful harvest of leaves and turn it into finished compost.

In addition to discussing what materials you can add to your pile, this chapter also delves into what tools you need to compost. From the most basic to the more advanced, these tools will make your life easier throughout the composting process. First, let's take a closer look at what you can compost.

Yard Trimmings

This includes anything you rake, cut, pull, and thin from your yard. Leaves, grass, unseeded weeds, excess plants, and anything else narrower than your pinkie finger make excellent compost fodder. For most people living around deciduous trees, leaves dropped from trees are the most abundant materials harvested from the yard.

What about the larger branches and woody-stalked plants? You can compost these, but large pieces of wood will take years to decompose. Unless you use a chipper shredder (see page 163), you will have to practice patience as you wait for branches to break down in a traditional backyard pile. Every year when you harvest, you will have to pull these mildly annoying sticks out from the rest of the compost.

However, larger twigs and woody plants can come in handy when you start a compost pile. Placing a layer of sticks on the bottom of a compost pile can add much-needed airflow up through the pile. Have the sticks going in different directions (think erratic Lincoln Logs) so they can support the mass of the pile without rolling out of the way.

Should you find yourself with a large amount of woody material and a nice sharp shovel, you could consider the Hugelkultur (pronounced *hoo-gul-culture*) method of composting described in Chapter 6. This integrated method of composting buries woody material under a raised garden bed, allowing the wood to slowly decompose over time. Alternatively, burn it in fireplace, give it away to neighbors, or send it off to your local yard waste program if you don't have much property.

Kitchen Scraps

This includes anything from a fruit or vegetable. Banana peels, apple cores, and stubs of lettuce all qualify. That slimy zucchini you forgot in the back of the produce drawer? Throw it in the compost!

Don't forget perhaps the best "scraps" coming from your kitchen: coffee grounds. These moist, nitrogen-rich spent coffee beans speed up your compost decomposition, smell fantastic, and ward off nosy critters from your bin. Disposable filters also break down, so toss the whole package in your kitchen collector. Coffee's less-strong-but-still-delicious beverage cousin, tea, also makes a great addition to your compost. Loose tea leaves and tea in bags can go into the pile. All parts of the tea bag except the very small staple will decompose. Since the chances of finding this tiny staple in finished compost are about as good as finding a needle in a haystack, I never remove staples from my tea bags.

Coffee grounds speed up decomposition in your compost bin.

Composting scraps from your kitchen turns your garbage into a valuable resource.

Always bury food scraps in your compost pile.

If you like to use a juicer at home, the pulp left from juicing your fruits and vegetables provides a nice kick of nitrogen to your pile and is already "prechewed," so it will break down quickly. Balance this high-nitrogen material with a good covering of shredded leaves.

Other kitchen scraps derived from plants, such as bread, rice, and crackers, can also go into a compost pile. Start composting these only after you have experience composting fruit and vegetable scraps. Cooked and processed scraps are more likely to have butter or oil, which you want to avoid, and breads and grains can create a garbagy smell in your bin if not composted correctly.

This leads to the most important rule of all: when composting kitchen scraps, always bury them with a generous layer of leaves. Use a garden fork to pull back a layer of the pile to hide the scraps under, or cover the food scraps with additional leaves after you add them. You should not be able to see broccoli stems or banana peels peeking out when you look into your pile. Burying your food scraps will eliminate odors and pesky fruit flies.

Backyard Chickens

IT'S OFFICIAL: you are no longer a weird hippie if you keep chickens in your backyard. Backyard chickens have become mainstream in many urban and suburban areas, providing their keepers not only with fresh eggs but also fresh manure. Each chicken will create 1 cubic foot of manure every six months. If you raise chickens, you can smell the high level of ammonia and know that you must clean up chicken manure regularly.

Fresh chicken manure is too strong for plants, so don't try to amend the soil by applying it directly. It could damage the plant roots or even kill the plant. That said, chicken manure makes an excellent addition to your compost pile. It contains more nitrogen, phosphorus, and potassium than most other domestic animal manures, and your micro- and macroorganism friends will break the manure down into usable compost.

Anyone using chicken manure in their compost should follow a few basic precautions to make sure any pathogens in the manure do not make you or your family sick.

1 Wear gloves when handling manure.

2 When using manure, practice hot composting techniques when possible to ensure the pile heats up enough to kill pathogens.

3 Never apply fresh manure to your plants. Only use manure that has been composted.

4 Thoroughly wash all vegetables planted in soil that you amended with compost derived from manure.

5 Anyone susceptible to foodborne illnesses (e.g. very young children or pregnant women) should avoid eating raw vegetables planted in soil that you amended with compost derived from manure.

As you read through the composting methods, chose one that heats up if you want to compost chicken manure. Do not use chicken manure in vermicomposting, trench composting, Bokashi, or indoor kitchen units. Turn the pile well to make sure all patches of the manure have experienced the heat stage. You also want to give compost derived from manure plenty of time to cure after the hot stage (at least two months). Your extra attention to this compost will be rewarded when you harvest the beautiful, crumbly black material high in nutrients for your plants.

Backyard chickens supply you with fresh eggs for the kitchen and fresh manure for your compost pile.

Herbivore Manure

Manure and bedding from animals that only eat plants make excellent additions to your compost pile. For the typical backyard composter, these animals include rabbits, gerbils, hamsters, and mice. Most domestic birds also create manure that you can easily compost in your backyard.

Aside from animals you keep as pets inside your home, you may have access to manure from farmed animals such as horses and goats. The high nitrogen content of all herbivore manure makes an excellent addition to your backyard compost, especially in the integrated composting techniques described in Chapter 6. Of course, anyone who has driven by a pig farm knows some manure smells better than others, so keep that and your neighbors in mind before you accept more manure than you can handle. A small amount of this high-nitrogen material will go a long way in a contained compost bin.

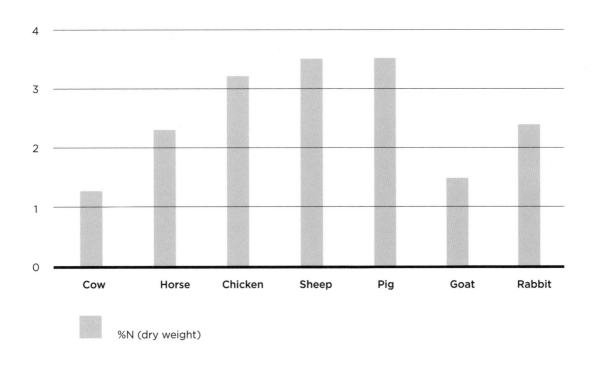

NITROGEN CONTENT OF DOMESTIC ANIMAL MANURES
%N (DRY WEIGHT)

%N (dry weight)

Source: "Organic Manures and Fertilizers for Vegetable Crops"

Stuff You Can Compost

Brown leaves	By far the most abundant material in our backyards (if you live in a temperate climate with deciduous trees), leaves provide a fantastic base for composting. Shred leaves if possible by running them over with a lawnmower or mulching mower.
Dead plants and flowers	Most garden plants will at some point have dead stalks or browning flowers to cut away. You can place any of these into your compost. For thicker stalks, consider chopping them into smaller pieces with garden shears or simply breaking them with your hands. Don't forget to toss in that wilted bouquet from inside your home as well.
Straw	Unless you decorate with straw or keep animals, you will probably have to outsource this material. Many grocery stores will have straw decorations in the fall and gratefully give it away once the "harvest" look is out and the Christmas decorations come in style.
Pine needles	We often just leave pine needles where they fall under evergreen trees or shrubs since they are so small. This practice works well to discourage weeds growing underneath. But occasionally, pine needles find their way onto walking paths or driveways where you sweep them up. Natural Christmas trees will also often shed needles. Wear gloves when you toss pine needles into the compost pile; they are called needles for a reason.
Sawdust and wood chips	Super-fine, lovely smelling sawdust and wood chips will both decompose in your pile. Shredded wood decomposes faster than traditional wood chips because the process of shredding the wood opens more crevices for our composting friends. One word of caution: stay away from sawdust created when cutting plywood. The glue in plywood contains phenol-formaldehyde, a potentially toxic substance.
Shredded newspaper	Oftentimes, especially toward the end of summer, we run out of brown leaves to add to our compost, and shredded newspaper offers a nice replacement. Unshredded newspaper will mat when wet, which is fine if you just want the paper to act like a cover on top of other material. Shredded paper decomposes faster and incorporates better with the other material.
Small pieces of brush and shrubs	Occasional small branches or cuttings of hardier plants will decompose fine in your compost. If you add too many, you may have to practice patience waiting for your final product.

Wood ash	Ash leftover from fires in a fire pit or fireplace will decompose in your compost pile and offer a unique composition of minerals and potash (potassium carbonate) to your finished compost. Add wood ash with caution, however. This material is very basic, and if you add too much at once, it could change the pH of your pile, essentially giving an eviction notice to your microorganisms. Just sprinkle a little at a time and everyone will be happier.
Cornstalks and husks	If you grow corn in your backyard, you likely will have a mess of stalks after harvest. Chop them up before placing them in your compost. You can also add the finer husks when you shuck the corn.
Fruit and vegetable scraps	You can compost potato peels, apple cores, carrot stems, melon rinds, and any other part of a vegetable or fruit that you do not eat. Make sure to bury these food scraps under leaves to avoid attracting fruit flies and other pesky insects.
Bread, crackers, and pasta	Occasionally bread grows mold, crackers go stale, and cooked pasta gets slimy before we have a chance to eat them. All these items compost well. You can also compost rice, muffins, and cookies if needed. You must bury these items in your pile or you could create garbagy odors and attract unwanted guests.
Coffee grounds and filters	Coffee may be one of the most popular drinks around, and luckily the grounds provide a nice boost of nitrogen to the compost pile. You can toss in the grounds and the filter with no need to bury; coffee grounds have an unpleasant odor for most animals and will actually deter critters from sniffing around your bin.
Loose tea and tea bags	Loose tea is just small wet leaves that will decompose very quickly. Once used, you can toss the whole tea bag into your compost pile. The string and bag will decompose with the tea, and the small staple, while it will remain intact, will disappear into your finished compost.
Green grass	Grass clippings decompose very quickly and can often be left on the lawn if you follow the grasscycling steps in Chapter 6. If you prefer to rake them up, your compost pile will welcome this high-nitrogen material with open arms. Mix the green grass in with brown leaves if you have a large amount of clippings. Without mixing, the grass may form a thick mat and force out much-needed air.
Green plants	Unseeded weeds, thinned plants, and other cuttings provide a high-nitrogen material and usually a good deal of bulk to your pile. Just remember to balance any green plants you add with twice as much brown material.
Manure from herbivores	Animals that eat plants provide a rich supplement to your compost pile. For most of us, that includes small household pets such as hamsters, gerbils, guinea pigs, and mice. Of course, if you have access to horse manure or manure from other large animals, take advantage of this and add it to your compost.

Composting for Homebrewers

IF YOU ARE one of the intrepid folks brewing your own beer in your basement, spent grains make a great addition to your compost pile. After going through the malting and mashing process, brewers rinse the grain to pull out the sugary liquid that makes the beer. Grain fresh from this process should have a nice smell and still contain a little malt sugar leftover from the rinsing. Bacteria in your compost pile love this leftover sugar and will break down the spent grains faster than you can say *doppelbock*.

When adding spent grains to your compost, balance them out with a dry material to discourage your pile from getting too wet. If wet grains start to decompose without air, they take on a putrid, vomit-like smell best left to bathrooms in shady dive bars. Spread the grains out over your pile and mix in shredded leaves or even shredded newspaper to soak up the excess moisture. If you add spent grains regularly, you will likely never need to water your pile. You can just sit back with your microbrew and let the microorganisms in your pile get to work.

Shredded newspaper makes a great high-carbon substitute when brown leaves become scarce.

Stuff You Shouldn't Compost

Putting the wrong materials into your compost can cause garbagy odors, attract pests such as flies or rodents, and even cause a health risk. Here is a list of what you should not put in your bin:

Meat and dairy products	In nature, animals decompose with no issues, but it is generally a smelly, bug-filled process. Adding meat to your compost bin will attract raccoons, rats, and other critters while also creating odors that no one, except maybe house flies, wants to smell. Meat and dairy also take a longer time to decompose than fruit and vegetable scraps.
Fish or fish parts	You may hear of intrepid gardeners using fish parts in their compost, but using fish in your compost is very high-level composting. You run the risk of serious odors (have you smelled rotting fish?) and attracting all the raccoons within a five-mile radius. This is not worth the risk.
Bones	There is a reason that every movie depicting a long-dead character shows them as a skeleton; bones last a long time. They will not decompose in your backyard compost pile without a serious amount of time or heat. Better to leave this tough item out.
Grease, oil, and fat	In the spirit of keeping our microinvertebrate friends happy, you should also avoid fat, oil, grease, and salad dressing as much as possible. These materials occupy much-needed air spaces while decomposing slowly and creating a garbage-like odor.
Charcoal ash or briquettes	Charcoal ash from your grill could contain chemicals harmful to your soil. If the briquettes have a binding chemical or a chemical to help the briquette burn, you should leave it out of your pile. Charcoal from pure wood poses no danger (once it has cooled) and will compost fine.
Diseased plants	When you know a disease has killed a plant, do not add the material to the compost. The disease could be pervasive, or your pile might not heat up enough to kill the disease. Risking further spread of the disease around your garden is not worth the finished compost you gain from those materials.
Weed seeds (see page 46)	Seeds from weeds could live through the compost process and spread themselves with your finished compost. Add weeds at your own risk.

Dog or cat manure	Dog and cat poop can contain harmful pathogens that your pile may not get hot enough to kill. It is also, needless to say, stinky. You also want to avoid adding manure from any other meat-eating pets, such as ferrets, snakes, or even the random kinkajou.
Plants harmful to humans	Some composters may disagree with this point, but I do not compost materials such as poison ivy in my backyard. I send it off with the yard trimmings collection my city offers. Pretty much all I have to do is look at this sneaky, three-leaved plant and I break out in blistering, horribly itchy hives. Keeping this out of my compost pile is just common sense. My backyard composting ban also applies to poison ivy's nasty cousins, including poison oak and poison sumac. They can all go back to the fiery depths of hell from whence they came. Other plants that could hurt you in the compost are those with thorns or other spiky features. I generally send cuttings from rose bushes or raspberry bushes to the curbside collection as well. The risk is yours to take.

Composting Weeds and Invasive Plants

Composting weeds is a matter of personal preference. I say the more the merrier when it comes to adding material to the compost bin. My philosophy is that those dandelion puffballs spread seeds through the air no matter how meticulously I try to avoid them. Why not throw your harvested weeds into the compost to reap the benefits of all that nitrogen?

On the other hand, I know some composters who dutifully separate out weeds with seeds from other yard trimmings so the seeds will not end up in their finished compost. You cannot guarantee that those seeds will get hot enough to decompose completely in the pile. As you spread your finished compost, you could also be spreading weed seeds (now in the perfect growing medium). To me, it is a risk worth taking, but you will have to decide for yourself.

A few invasive plants (depending on where you live) will not die in your compost pile, and I recommend you do not include those for nature's sake. The buttercup is one such plant where I live. Such a sweet, unassuming looking plant—but it will take over in no time. Check with your local agricultural extension office for a list of the invasive plants in your area.

Growing Plants for Composting

Most of the materials you place in your pile represent the "leftovers"—the peel of the banana, the core of the apple, the dying flower stems after a bloom, or the leaves falling from trees. Some composters take gardening a step further and incorporate varieties of plants into their garden that are especially good for the compost bin. Some plants, such as legumes, fix nitrogen from the air into the soil and end up holding a good deal of nitrogen in their leaves, seeds, roots, and stems. Other plants for a compost garden act as cover crops when a bed is not in use.

Consider integrating these plants into your garden plans and then harvesting them for your compost:

Red clover or yellow sweet clover

Alfalfa

Cereal rye

Kale

Daikon radishes

Black-eyed peas

Comfrey

Borage

Borage and red kale are great for compost and lend interesting color and varied height to this raised-bed garden.

Can I Compost Black Walnut Leaves?

IF YOU RUN in social circles with serious gardeners, you have probably received warnings of the deadly effects of black walnut trees. Black walnut trees create a chemical called "juglone" that is toxic to many plants we grow, such as tomatoes, blueberries, and azaleas. If you happen to have one of these beautiful trees in your yard, you may wonder if the leaves from black walnut trees create a toxic compost, causing your favorite plants to bite the dust.

It turns out that you can add the leaves to your compost with no worries. The toxin in these leaves breaks down within two to four weeks of composting. Let the leaves thoroughly break down in your compost bin and you'll be fine.

Woodchips and nut shells from the black walnut do require a longer period to decompose, so give them at least six months to a year to break down before using the finished compost. Do not use this wood in the Hugelkultur method of slow composting described in Chapter 6. If the compost still makes you nervous, test a little of the finished compost by using it to plant a few tomato plant seedlings and see if they survive. If sacrificial experiments are not your thing, you can always use the finished compost on the many plants not sensitive to our black walnut friends, such as Japanese maple or clematis.

Untraditional Compostables

Aside from fruit and veggie scraps and yard trimmings, you will come across a motley assortment of items that you can toss into a compost bin. As you become more and more experienced/obsessed with composting, you'll probably find more to add to this list:

Cotton swabs (cotton/cardboard swabs only—no plastic!)

Eggshells

Tissues

Dryer lint

Paper towels

Pet hair

Human hair

Matches (extinguished and cooled, of course)

Nail clippings

Soy milk and almond milk

Nut shells

Tofu

Old wine and beer

Urine

Feathers from old pillows

Vacuum cleaner dust

Old potting soil

Pee?! Really?!

OUR LOCAL SOIL and water conservation district conducted a study that sampled finished compost from seven different residential compost piles. One sample stood out as having a much higher level of available nitrogen than the others (327 ppm versus the average of 110 ppm). When they asked the homeowner how he created such fantastically balanced compost, he sheepishly admitted to regularly peeing on the leaf pile.

Yes, urine (both pet and human) makes a fantastic addition to a compost pile. High in nitrogen, urine acts as an accelerator to help carbon-rich dry leaves decompose faster. How you get the urine to the compost pile, well, that's up to you.

Dryer lint will quickly disappear in a compost bin.

Balancing Browns and Greens

One of the most fundamental skills a backyard composter learns is how to balance brown and green material. Too many green items and you will end up with a stinky mess. Too many brown items and your pile will decompose slower than a herd of turtles stampeding through peanut butter.

You need to add about three parts brown material to every one part green material to get the magic balance of carbon and nitrogen that leads to a fast and odor-free decomposition process.

So how do you tell the difference between green and brown? Brown materials are rich in carbon, meaning they have a much higher carbon content compared with nitrogen.

Green materials have a relatively higher percentage of nitrogen than the brown materials. The nitrogen helps speed up the decomposition of the brown materials.

Add about three-fourths stuff from the brown pile and about one-fourth stuff from the green pile. Don't worry about pulling out the scale or the measuring cups. Do what experienced composters do: "eyeball" the proportions. You really gain an intuitive feel for the right balance the more you compost. Remember, composting is forgiving, and these items will break down regardless of how much you add. If you tend to geek out over numbers and want to explore carbon to nitrogen ratios further, check out the tables on page 31.

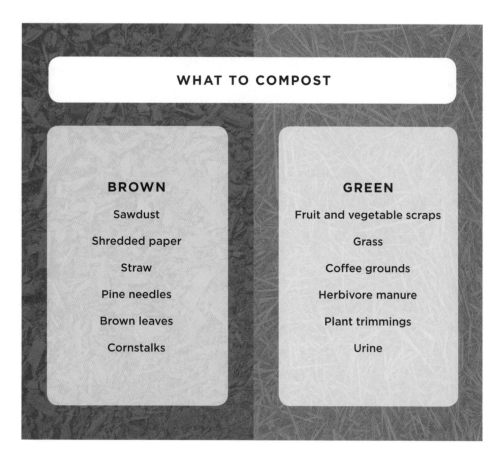

WHAT TO COMPOST

BROWN

Sawdust

Shredded paper

Straw

Pine needles

Brown leaves

Cornstalks

GREEN

Fruit and vegetable scraps

Grass

Coffee grounds

Herbivore manure

Plant trimmings

Urine

Add three parts brown materials to every one part green materials to maintain a balanced compost pile.

Keeping Material Small

Our microinvertebrate friends will eat any organic thing you throw in the compost bin, but if you want them to eat faster, make the pieces smaller. Chopping up the material increases the surface area for the bacteria and fungi. It's like opening up more rooms for your party so you can fit more friends. Chopping up large (hello, pumpkins) or dense (look out, broccoli stalks) material will help your microorganisms create finished compost in much less time.

Tools for Composting

Like gardening tools, some composting tools hold more importance than others, and their degree of importance is a matter of personal preference. Think of these first few tools as your "starter kit." Yes, you can compost without them, but they make life much easier.

Chopping scraps you do not want to eat into smaller pieces will help them decompose faster.

Basic Composting Tools (The Starter Kit)

COMPOST BIN

While not essential (as you will see in Chapter 6), a compost bin acts as a vessel to keep material contained and protected. Compost bins come in many shapes and sizes, and Chapter 5 will help you select one suitable for your yard and lifestyle.

AERATOR

To maintain the best environment for our microorganism friends, we have to give them plenty of air to breathe. Otherwise, the anaerobic cousins move in and the neighborhood goes downhill. An aerator will let you easily add air to the pile with less work than a pitchfork. One end of the aerator generally has a handle, and the other end connects to an auger-type device that fluffs up the compacted parts of the pile, leaving air pockets in its wake. Some aerators twist down into the pile, while others plunge in and have blades that open up and pull in air on the ascent.

A good aerator will be sturdy, easy to clean, and slim enough to make poking in the pile manageable. You might need to put your back into it, but your work will be rewarded when your pile almost immediately starts heating up and reducing in size.

Resourceful composters can find substitutes for an official aerator in other supplies from the garage or toolshed. A piece of rebar or a sturdy stick with a pointy end will do the aeration job in a pinch. See page 66 for plans for creating a DIY auger from very inexpensive supplies.

Organic Composting

WHEN PEOPLE SAY "organic," they throw out a word with a variety of meanings. In this book, we have so far used *organic* to mean anything that was once or still is alive. Organic matter breaks down in our compost bins, unlike rock, glass, plastic, or metal, which does not break down (or breaks down so slowly that it would not decompose in our lifetimes).

In popular culture, *organic* means grown or created without certain chemical pesticides or fertilizers that could be harmful for our bodies or the environment. I'm not here to debate the benefits of organic versus nonorganic lifestyles, but I do meet composters interested in creating purely "organic" compost without adding materials that could contain pesticides or fertilizers.

If you share a similar interest, just be diligent about adding materials that have been certified organic or that you know are free of the chemicals you are trying to avoid. For example, if your neighbor sees you compost and generously offers a bag of fresh grass, you might want to ask if he uses chemicals on his lawn. If you need to add shredded paper because your brown leaf stock is depleted, make sure the paper is organic and the inks are plant-based. If you go organic in your grocery shopping, most of the food scraps you add likely carry the organic label too.

Most pesticides and fertilizers are designed to break down quickly, so only concern yourself with "organic" composting if you consider this important in other aspects of your life, such as the food you eat or the clothes you purchase. Interestingly, I do find that most composters naturally move away from chemical fertilizers and pesticides as they reap the benefits of using compost in their own backyard and find they no longer need them.

This well-constructed three-unit compost bin has a locking lid and special doors at the bottom for easier harvesting.

PITCHFORK OR SPADING FORK

Nothing moves manure and wet compost better than a pitchfork. The tines of the fork slice through the compost while the wetness of the materials hold the clump you scooped up together on the pitchfork. Unless the compost is very dry, you will exert less effort using a pitchfork than a spade or a shovel. When my husband gave me my first pitchfork as a present (yes, I am that kind of girl), I felt like I was joining some special agrarian club reserved for only serious composters and farmers.

All pitchforks are not the same. People use different pitchforks for different functions. Some pitchforks have special designs specifically to make scooping up animal manure easier. They come in an impressive variety of styles ranging from simple manure forks to models that look like giant scoops for your cat litter box. Unless you have large animals depositing copious amounts of

manure, you do not need one of the very specialized types of pitchforks. A simple manure fork will work fine for compost purposes.

The term *pitchfork* traditionally describes pitchforks with more delicate tines designed to scoop lightweight material like straw or hay, such as the one featured in the iconic *American Gothic* painting. These slender tines could bend under the heavier weight of compost.

What I use—and what most gardeners call a pitchfork—is technically a spading fork. These very tough tools generally have four strong tines and a robust wooden handle. They take a beating with no complaint. You can dig into rocky earth, scoop mountains of manure and compost, and aerate rocky soil with a spading fork. I know I shouldn't call a spading fork a pitchfork, but I just can't break the habit. When I refer to a pitchfork in this book, a spading fork is the tool I have in mind.

A good, sturdy wheelbarrow helps distribute harvested compost around the garden.

WHEELBARROW

A wheelbarrow comes in handy for many garden tasks and becomes especially helpful when you harvest your compost. Slightly wet, heavy, and plentiful finished compost simply must be proudly paraded around your yard in a wheelbarrow. Sometimes I admire my wheelbarrow of finished compost just for fun before spreading it around my garden.

Of course, a garden cart with two wheels will also work well for this purpose. Garden carts seem to come in larger sizes, so you may prefer a cart if you have a larger yard.

In a pinch, you can carry your compost in 5-gallon buckets. Considering people invented the wheelbarrow nearly 2,000 years ago, I suggest utilizing the tool that's been used for generations and saving the bucket for the light-duty kitchen work.

KITCHEN COLLECTOR

A designated vessel to collect scraps in your kitchen will make you much more likely to actually compost your food scraps. These come in fancy stainless-steel or bamboo models, or they can be as simple as a plastic bucket. Kitchen collectors act as a reminder to everyone else in your house to place that banana peel in the compost pail instead of the trash.

Think about whether you want your kitchen collector to reside on the counter, under the counter, or on the floor next to your garbage can. Personal preference will dictate your degree of fanciness, but you could even reuse an old coffee can (some even have aroma-lock technology) or an old butter tub. Fruit flies travel into your home on produce from the grocery store, so having a lid will help deter those pesky critters from living in your scraps. A handle is also nice but not essential.

If you want the coolest kitchen collector on the block, you can purchase one with a carbon filtration system embedded in the lid. This thin carbon filter allows the scraps to breathe but blocks any offensive odors until you can empty the contents into the compost pile.

A kitchen collector makes collecting food scraps easier.

SHOVEL OR SPADE

Probably the most basic tool on our list, a good sharp shovel (sometimes called a spade) could be your best friend in the garden and when you compost. I drag both my pitchfork and shovel with me when I harvest my compost and use my shovel to distribute the compost around my garden, usually as mulch. If you plan on using any of the integrated composting techniques in Chapter 6, your shovel will be by your side.

I prefer a sharp square-headed shovel for most of my work with compost. It provides a good surface area for scooping and can slice into dense, moist compost when necessary. For digging down into heavy clay soil for trench composting or to amend your soil with compost, you may prefer a pointed shovel. Chances are you already have a shovel or spade preference and have several of these indispensable tools in your tool shed.

GLOVES

Gloves may not technically fall into the tool category, but you should wear them when you harvest compost or come into contact with unfinished compost when aerating. Not only do they protect your hands from blisters, but they also protect you from harmful fungi or pathogens that occasionally turn up in a hard-working compost pile.

LEAF RAKE

These wide, semiflexible rakes provide the perfect sweeping action to gather leaves for your compost pile. Leaves make up the majority of most compost piles and are probably the most abundant compost fodder we encounter. A leaf rake also comes in handy if you want to use your finished compost to amend the soil under your grass. It gently works the compost between the blades and down into the soil.

PRUNERS

You likely use pruners or loppers to work in your yard, but these tools work well for breaking up tougher materials before composting them. Breaking up twigs and vines into shorter pieces not only makes them decompose faster, but it also makes aeration easier since they are less likely to tangle up around your aerator.

Reducing Odors from Your Kitchen Collector

LET'S FACE IT: sometimes life gets away from us and we don't always have time to take the kitchen scraps to the compost bin every day. Especially in the winter, I will trek out to the bin juggling several bowls with three or four days' worth of material. If odors from kitchen scraps concern you—or if fruit flies bother you in the summer—you can take a few preemptive measures.

Some composters keep a small pail of sawdust next to their kitchen pail. Every time they add food scraps, they also sprinkle sawdust on top. This helps soak up extra liquids and keeps the pail smelling fresh.

Composters also can now purchase biochar, a relatively recent product in the composting world, to help reduce kitchen-collector odors. Biochar is a high-carbon product created by heating organic materials such as grass and wood in a manner that doesn't burn them but transforms the material. Some gardeners use biochar in combination with compost as a fertilizer for their garden, but you can also use it in the kitchen to act as a type of carbon filter for your scraps. Simply sprinkle some biochar on top of the food scraps every time you add them.

Advanced Composting Tools

These are tools that, while not essential, will make your composting experience a bit more professional.

SCREENER

When I first started composting, I never screened my finished compost. It seemed like an unnecessary step. Why not just work the finished compost into the soil and be done? Well, that was before I experienced the mind-blowing satisfaction of seeing my own finished compost perfectly screened.

Composting is a waiting game. You regularly add materials, turn the pile, and water if needed, but it takes months, sometimes a year, to actually see the results. That finished compost is your creation, the best soil amendment around made by you from your "garbage." You should be proud. Now imagine taking that proud product and further refining it through screening. You end up with stunningly beautiful compost, better than anything you would find in a garden store.

Screening pulls out the peach pits, unfinished clumps of unidentifiable muck, sticks, and sometimes even produce stickers. All the unfinished stuff can go back into your compost bin as treasure for another day. (See page 163 for DIY screener instructions.)

HAND CULTIVATOR OR GARDEN FORK

Reaching into your compost with bare hands is usually a risky proposition. Those seemingly benign leaves could be hiding a gooey, rotten melon filled with maggots. If you would rather not play Russian roulette with your compost pile, invest in a small hand cultivator or garden fork. This handheld tool acts like an extension of your hand, allowing you to pull back the top layer of the pile and neatly tuck the food scraps in for their nap. I keep one next to my compost bin and use it every day when adding scraps to the pile.

CHIPPER SHREDDER

Some yard tools are not so fun (I'm looking at you, leaf rake), but others can actually bring a satisfied grin to your face. Using a chipper shredder will have you smiling. These electric- or gas-powered machines have a funnel-like chute ending in a metal-bladed grinder that spins to shred whatever you throw in there. Residential models can turn a branch measuring 3 inches in diameter into mulch, perfect for using around the yard or adding to your compost pile as a source of carbon. Most models claim around a 20-to-1 reduction in size.

Aside from branches, you can also shred your leaves before composting them. Shredding leaves dramatically reduces how long they take to decompose.

Most home chipper shredders cost between $200 and $1,000, depending on how much horsepower you want and how large of a branch you hope to destroy. As much fun as these tools are to use, please follow all safety precautions; these machines are serious tools, and as anyone who has seen *Fargo* remembers, they can grind hands and arms just as easily as branches.

If an expensive chipper shredder is not in your budget, a regular mulching mower will chop up your leaves nicely. Just run over the leaves with the mower, and they will compost much more quickly in your bin. A leaf vacuum or strong garden trimming tool will also shred leaves well.

COMPOST THERMOMETER

If the science of composting fascinates you or if you gain satisfaction from watching the compost thermometer register your pile as 140°F, buy yourself a compost thermometer. You certainly do not need one to tell you your steaming compost is hot, but it does give you an actual number to brag about to all your fellow composters. You can use a thermometer to tell you when the compost enters each stage so you can judge if you need to turn the pile and how long you have to wait for finished compost.

Shredded leaves break down much faster than whole leaves.

KITCHEN COLLECTOR LINERS

You can buy small biodegradable bags to go inside your compost pail made of a plastic supposedly designed to break apart in your backyard bin. Purchase these at your own risk. The ones I have tried performed poorly at best, very slowly breaking down and causing a headache as I speared them while aerating. Pulling a plastic bag full of decomposed food scraps off an aerator is not my idea of fun.

The concept behind these bags—keeping your kitchen collector clean—appeals to me, though.

When you empty your kitchen pail, you almost always have carrot peels or a few strawberry tops stubbornly hanging onto the bottom. Very wet materials sometimes create a stinky compost stew at the bottom of the bucket. A liner creates a barrier between your food scraps and the pail and makes cleaning your kitchen collector much easier. If you want to line your kitchen collector with something that will actually decompose, consider making your own liners out of newspaper. With a few minutes of newspaper origami, you will create a nice stack of bucket liners that will last for several weeks.

In-Kitchen Composting Machines

HUMAN INGENUITY is constantly at work, looking to solve our everyday problems and make our lives easier. Home composting certainly benefits from this continuous improvement as evidenced by the in-kitchen composting machines recently seen on the market. These gadgets, although pricey, can supply home composters with a valuable service to speed up composting.

Imagine if you had someone in your kitchen who would take your food scraps, chop them into little pieces for you, and then bake them while frequently mixing the scraps to ensure perfect dehydration. This person also regularly fans the scraps to guarantee they create no odors. Basically, this is what you get when you spend a few hundred bucks on an in-kitchen composting machine.

Different models obviously have different methods of working and also promise varied end products.

For example, one model claims to speed up composing to just a few weeks, regularly adding heat, mixing the contents, and pushing in air to create a soil amendment. Another basically acts as a dehydrator, macerating and heating the scraps until they look like brown, crispy pieces of lovely compost. This model claims to give you compost in three hours.

Make no mistake, these in-kitchen composters do not create compost. They heat the material to temperatures above what our microbe friends can sustain, essentially sterilizing the food scraps. The models claiming to give you finished compost in a few hours are only dehydrating your food scraps into small, dry, sterile pieces. If you place this material outside, it will soak up rain to rehydrate and then finish the decomposition process.

Although they do not finish the compost, they do process the food scraps into a useful form. If you consider these devices as precomposting, food-scrap-preparation tools, then they really can speed up decomposition in your pile. The simple act of breaking material into smaller pieces is quite valuable in decreasing the time it takes the microbes in your pile to break down food scraps.

On the same premise that I refuse to buy an electric toothbrush when I can just move my arm back and forth, I would not purchase a device that uses electricity to do something I can do with a pitchfork and a few billion of my closest microbe friends. This decision falls into the realm of personal preference. If you or someone in your family dislike the ick factor of rotting food scraps or if you just love gadgets, I can see the appeal of using one of these machines.

DIY KITCHEN COLLECTOR LINER

This simple liner will keep your food scraps contained in a nice package, soak up excess liquids, and act as a source of carbon when you toss the package in the compost bin. You will never again have to bang the kitchen pail on the side of your compost bin while attempting to dislodge potato peels and tea leaves stuck to the bottom.

Materials Needed:

1 Black-and-white newspaper
2 Scissors (or excellent tearing skills)

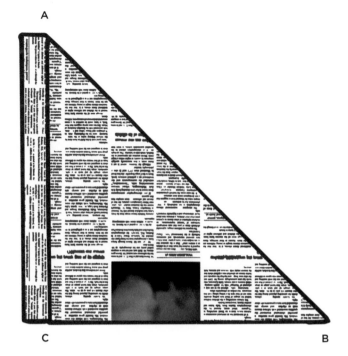

Follow these simple instructions to create a compost pail liner out of newspaper.

Let's Do It ➜

1
Stack three or four pieces of newspaper together.

2
Fold one corner down to the opposite edge to create a triangle.

3
Cut the excess newspaper off the triangle. (If you were to unfold the triangle, it would make a square.) Your creased line should connect corner A and corner B.

4
Fold one of the corners on your crease (corner A) to the corner opposite of the crease (corner C). The corner opposite of the crease is bordered by two free sides.

5
Fold the other corner on the crease (corner B) down to the same opposite corner. You should now have a square.

6
Unfold the last two pieces so your newspaper forms a triangle again. You will use the crease lines as guides for your next step.

7
Fold one of the corners (A) bordering the original fold down to the center of the other side. The crease you just unfolded will guide you to that point.

8
Fold the other corner (B) bordered by the original fold over to the center of the opposite side. The crease you unfolded in Step 6 will again act as a guide to indicate the center point of that side.

9
Now find the last point of your triangle, the only corner (C) with free paper on either side. Fold several layers of paper down over the other paper to create an opening. Fold the rest of the layers down on the other side.

10
Open up the area you just folded back and you have a paper liner. Alternatively, you can also use this to create a very fashionable hat.

DIY liner instructions come from Green Bin Ottawa.

4

MAINTAINING YOUR COMPOST BIN

WHAT KIND OF COMPOSTER ARE YOU?

In the broad spectrum of people who compost, you will find a range of drastically varied behaviors. On one end are the fanatic active composters who turn their bin every other day and seek out more compost fodder for an ever-increasing harvest. On the other end of the spectrum live the lazy, just-let-it-rot composters who are content to allow Mother Nature to do her thing. Of course, most of us fall somewhere in between the two extremes, and how much time you put into the maintenance of your compost will vary accordingly.

This chapter gives you the concepts you need to successfully set up and maintain your pile of rotting stuff and turn it into brown gold. Whether you spend five minutes a week or five hours a week is up to you. Let's dive deeper into how to set up and maintain your backyard composting oasis.

Location, Location, Location: Finding Just the Right Spot

When scouting your yard for a composting location, look for the following qualities:

- Protection from too much sun or wind
- Good drainage
- Easy access from your home

A sunny spot will help heat up your pile, but intense sunlight could also cause your pile to dry out. I find that shady or partially sunny spots require less maintenance—especially watering—in the long run. A pile with the right balance of brown and green will heat up even in the shadiest of locations. Like too much sun, too much wind can also dry out your pile, so consider the exposure of an area to strong winds before setting up your compost.

While you may want your pile to stay moist, too much water can cause catastrophe. Choose a location that drains well and does not hold water when it rains. Standing water will create a mucky, smelly mess in your compost. A good way to scope out an area's drainage is to watch what happens during and after a rainfall. If a spot forms a small pond when it rains, avoid setting up a compost pile in that spot, or your backyard may start smelling like a swamp.

Imagine it is late at night and you are cleaning up your kitchen in your slippers. You happen to glance at your overflowing food scrap bucket and realize you still need to take your kitchen scraps to the compost bin. Is your location close enough to the house to allow a quick trot from your door to the bin? What about in the winter? Will you still be able to make the trek then? Locating the pile conveniently close to the house increases your chances of following through on adding those precious food scraps to your pile even when you are busy or in less-than-ideal weather. If your bin lives too far away from your back door, you may decide not to make the trip and pitch those valuable food scraps in the trash.

You will save future stress by avoiding these potential problem areas:

- Near trees (especially small or medium trees)
- Against a wood fence
- Directly next to your home

When I purchased my first home, I placed my backyard compost bin in an out-of-the way space near my property line. The spot seemed perfectly cozy under a medium-sized tree that stood in my neighbor's yard. During the first harvest, I learned why placing a compost bin directly under a tree is a bad idea. I had created beautiful compost, but the neighboring tree wanted to share in the harvest and had grown its roots up into the pile. I spent hours battling and hacking (sorry, tree) at roots to pull any usable compost from my bin. After that disaster, I decided to move my bin to the other side of the yard, out of the reach of any overeager trees. Very large trees with deep roots don't seem to have the same inclination to steal your compost.

Wood fences may seem like a natural fit to act as one side of your compost bin, but that will also lead to problems. Compost bins decompose organic matter, and your wood fence is organic matter even if it is treated or painted. Eventually, that fence will become part of the compost pile and decompose. My guess is that your neighbor would be none-too-happy if your compost started peeking through the fence to say hello. Leave at least a foot of space in between your bin and a wood fence.

For a similar reason, you also want to avoid placing your compost bin directly next to your home. The process of composting encourages bugs of all sorts. While we are happy to create that space for the crawling critters in the compost bin, we do not want to invite them inside our homes. Place your compost in a spot easily accessible from your back door but with enough distance (10 feet at least) to discourage any unwanted house guests.

Shredding leaves and yard trimmings will speed up how fast they decompose.

Off to a Successful Start

Once you have a bin and a location, you will be eager to get the party, otherwise known as the compost pile, started. Beginning with a few feet of shredded brown leaves will give your pile a nice base layer from which to grow. Shredded leaves will break down much faster, but if time is not an issue for you, adding whole leaves works too.

If you collect kitchen scraps, dump the scraps on top of a few feet of leaves and then cover them with more leaves (you should not be able to see any scraps peeking out). Add weeds you pull from the yard or small trimmings from plants as you have them. Sprinkle on a shovelful of healthy garden soil (not the sterile stuff you buy in a bag) on top of the pile to jumpstart the decomposing organisms. Keep bringing out your food scraps and burying them with leaves, and soon micro- and macroorganisms will have populated the pile, rip-roaring your compost into action.

1   Start with a few feet of brown leaves (shredding optional).
2   Add kitchen scraps and bury with more leaves.
3   Add plant trimmings from the yard.
4   Sprinkle with healthy garden soil.

Maintaining Air Pockets in Your Compost

We've already discussed our friends in depth—the aerobic, air-loving microorganisms that perform the bulk of the work in turning our "garbage" into luscious, wonderful compost. One of the essential needs of our air-loving friends is, of course, air. The more food scraps and leaves you add to the pile, the more the weight compacts the layers, pushing out the air pockets our friends need to do their job. In order to keep our aerobic microorganisms happy, we must add air back in. Adding air gives the microorganisms room to multiply and speeds up decomposition. How do we get air into a giant pile of stuff?

If you have a tumbler, aeration is simple: a quick spin of the bin gives you all the air you need. If you have a two- or three-unit setup designed for moving piles from one unit to the next, then your pitchfork and back muscles will be adding air on a regular basis. Having a multiple-unit composter or a pile gives you the advantage of "easy" pile turning using a pitchfork. The act of moving compost from one side to the next (or moving it from one spot to the next with an open pile) gives the compost a nice boost of oxygen.

Starting Small: How to Take Baby Steps into Composting

IF YOU HAVE never composted before or you had a bad experience in the past, starting with a basic compost pile allows you to get used to composting with little risk of an odor catastrophe. Begin with a few feet of shredded leaves and add coffee grounds occasionally. The coffee gives the leaves a nice kick of nitrogen. A simple brown-leaf-and-coffee-ground pile will yield fantastic results, and you may be content to keep your backyard composting at this basic level.

If you have mastered the basic and yearn for more, you can move on to adding fruit and vegetable scraps to the bin. Always bury your food scraps under leaves. You can also begin adding plant trimmings from around your yard. The more confident you feel in your composting ability, the more you can expand your list until you have reached master composter status.

If you have a single-bin unit, the two most commonly used techniques are aerating the pile manually or adding materials that discourage the pile from compacting. A third, less-often-employed method is to engineer the pile to pull air in using PVC plumbing pipes. We will examine each technique in turn so you can choose the best for you.

Aerating the Pile

For the traditional black plastic bin with an open bottom, using a specialized aerating tool will help you create air pockets in just a few minutes of stabbing. Aerating tools generally have a sharp end and little metal or plastic flaps that protrude out as you pull the tool up. A pointy stick would also help add some air into the pile; you just have to do a little more stabbing than with the specialized tools. Depending on your day, you may find stabbing something with a pointy stick quite therapeutic.

After you turn the pile, you will notice the compost heating up and decreasing in size over the next few days or weeks. Take this as a good sign that your pile is doing what it is supposed to do.

You can choose how eager or lazy you want to be with your compost when it comes to aeration. Once a week will earn you an A and finished compost in a few short months. Once-a-month aeration also works well, and you will have finished compost in nine months to a year. I know lazy composters who never turn their piles and still harvest beautiful compost. You do run the risk of the pile going anaerobic by not turning it, but everyone's backyard, neighbors, and lifestyles are different.

An aeration tool is the easiest way to add air and speed up decomposition.

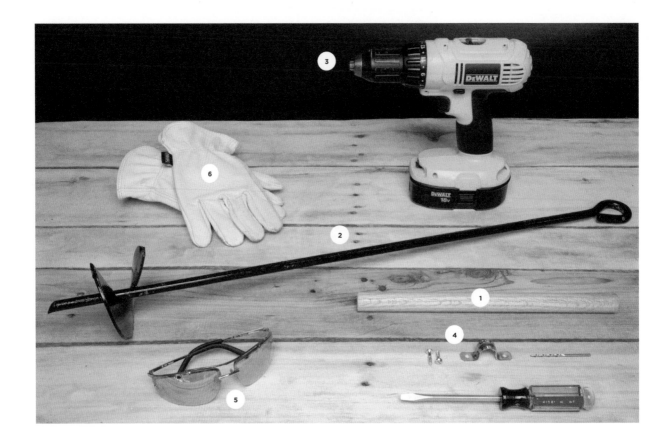

DIY COMPOST AERATOR

Remember in elementary school when teachers would say, "You can do anything if you put your mind to it"? Have you ever considered making your own tool? Believe me when I say that for a few dollars in parts and a super-easy assembly, this little auger is worth considering. You can do this.

Augers act like large corkscrews that spiral down through your compost pile to create a nice path for much-needed air. They require a little work (more if your pile is really dense). Like weeding or cleaning your bathroom, this job is easier if you do it on a regular basis, such as once per week, rather than waiting until your pile is an unmovable mass that only the Incredible Hulk would be able to aerate.

Ground anchors are available in most home improvement stores and also at camper or mobile home supply stores. You will find a variety of lengths; choose one that will reach deep into your pile but is not too heavy for you to lift. Brackets usually come with screws, so make sure you choose a package with screws that are shallow enough so they won't go all the way through the dowel.

Materials Needed:

1 Hardwood dowel
2 Auger-type ground anchor (about 3 feet in length)
3 Drill and screwdriver
4 Bracket and screws to secure
5 Eye protection
6 Work gloves

DIY COMPOST AERATOR

Let's Do It ➜

1
Measure and mark the center point of the dowel.

2
Place the wood dowel through the eye hole in the top of the ground anchor.

3
Set the bracket over the anchor and mark where the holes are on the dowel.

4
Remove the bracket and predrill holes. This will help prevent the dowel from splitting when you drill the screw holes.

5
Drill the holes for the screws based on the size of the screw that came with your bracket.

6
Reassemble the dowel, ground anchor, and bracket. Secure the bracket with screws.

If you want to gussy up your auger, polish the wood dowel with a sealer used for canoe paddles. To use the auger, simply push it into the compost bin. I like to create a grid in my mind and auger each section for more thorough aeration.

Auger plans created by a longtime gardener and tinkerer.

Creating Air Pockets with Materials

If using an aerator or pitchfork to turn the pile seems like too much work for you, adding materials that fluff up your pile is a nice alternative. Thin layers of sticks, straw, stalks, or other coarse material, especially at the bottom of a newly created pile, will allow pockets of air to form in the bin and act as a hangout spot for our favorite air-loving microorganisms. Sticks and other larger woody materials take a long time to decompose, so you may be pulling them out and throwing them back in at harvest time, but they help discourage materials from compacting and forcing air out of the pile.

Consider adding these items to help keep air in the pile:

Sticks
Plant stalks
Old straw
Wood chips
Paper towel cores
Egg cartons
Corn cobs

Sometimes you can use these items in conjunction with traditional aeration. If you use an aerator (an auger or stick with wings), however, layers of sticks will hamper your movement through the pile.

Engineering Aeration

If you know you will not have the time or willpower to aerate the pile, you can reap similar benefits by engineering a passive aeration system into your pile. It is not as complicated as it sounds and is more effective than adding materials to fluff up the pile. A PVC pipe with holes drilled every 6 inches can allow air to flow into the center of your pile and keep your microorganism friends active.

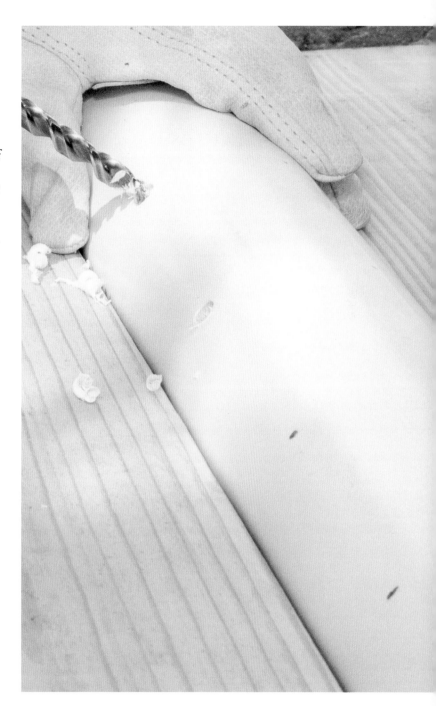

A PVC pipe with regular holes will bring air into your compost pile.

If you have an open pile or a wire bin, you can integrate horizontally laid PVC pipes into the pile as you build. Just make sure one or both ends are open to the outside air. Should you have a plastic or wooden bin, vertically place the pipe deep in your pile as close to the center as you can manage. As you mound material around the pipe and the pile starts to decompose, the air in the pipe heats up, and sometimes you can even feel warm air flowing out of the top opening.

Engineering airflow into your pile with PVC pipe is mostly a matter of tinkering and experimenting, so how-to instructions cannot provide much assistance. Still, some guidelines will help you get started:

- Keep at least one end of the pipe open to the air, both if possible. If you have a bin with a lid, cut the vertical pipe so that the lid can still fit on but the pile does not smother the top of the pipe.

- Following this method early in your compost pile's life allows you to build the pile around the pipe, which is much easier than trying to insert the pipe post pile construction (say that three times fast).

- Use PVC pipe with a diameter of at least 2 inches but no more than 6 inches. Anything larger will take up unnecessary space in your bin. Multiple small pipes work better than one large one.

- Drill holes about every 6 inches. You can also buy preperforated pipe and skip the drilling step.

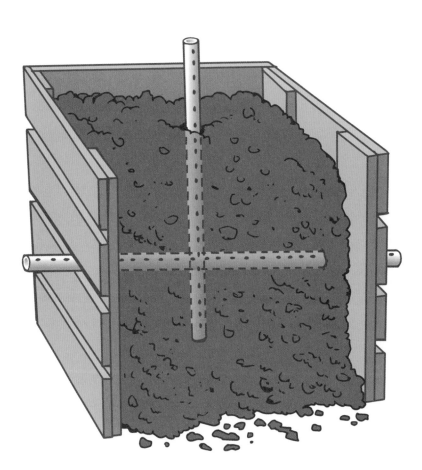

PVC pipes with holes allow air to flow into the pile, increasing the speed of decomposition.

As an alternative to PVC pipe, you can also use hardware cloth or chicken wire rolled into the shape of a cylinder. Not surprisingly, small bits of material will more easily migrate into these types of cylinders, and they tend to be more difficult to pull out of a pile than PVC, but they should still do the job. Make sure the wire roll is thick enough to have sufficient strength to withstand the crushing weight of the pile.

Passive aeration may cause your pile to take slightly longer to decompose than actively mixing it on a regular basis, but you will get a similarly successful outcome. When you are ready to harvest the compost, pull out the PVC pipes and grab your shovel or pitchfork to load up the wheelbarrow with brown gold.

Turning Versus Aerating

Many composters, myself included, are guilty of using the terms *aerating* and *turning* interchangeably. Some methods of aerating a pile also turn the materials, such as with a compost tumbler or with a multi-unit bin where you physically move the pile with a pitchfork. Most aeration techniques, including augers, simply supply air to the microorganisms in the pile.

Turning a compost pile moves the material on the outside of the pile into the hot center to more thoroughly decompose. Turning also ensures that those materials will reach a high temperature, killing weed seeds and pathogens. If you want faster decomposition, physically stir your materials at least once during your composting process. This may require removing the plastic compost bin off your pile and scoping everything back into the bin. Even without turning, your materials will eventually decompose, perhaps just not as quickly or evenly as possible.

Providing Your Compost with Water

Imagine our microorganism friend merrily munching on some nice dry leaves in your pile just like you would munch on a bowl of potato chips. After a while, he will need something to wash down those leaves. He can't reach for a tall glass of iced tea like you can. What is our friend to do?

All life on earth requires water to survive, and nature makes no exception for our compost organisms. The trick to backyard composting is to know how much water our buddies need and when we need to add more. Your compost pile should feel as wet as a wrung-out sponge. If you pick up (wearing gloves) a handful of compost matter and squeeze, that material should not release more than a few drops of water. If the compost crackles in your hands into a dry crispiness, it needs water. If you can squeeze a shower out of the compost with your hands, then the pile has too much water.

The simple act of adding food scraps likely supplies your compost with all necessary water most of the year. However, if you live in a very hot climate or if it's the peak heat of summer, adding water to your pile will help keep your microorganisms alive. In order to avoid the chlorinated water coming from most hoses, first fill a bucket with water and allow the chlorine a few hours to evaporate before watering your pile. You can also use water from your rain barrel if you have one.

Should you find your pile too wet, add dry leaves or shredded paper to help soak up the water. Leaving the lid off (if you have one) will also help the excess moisture escape as long as Mother Nature does not decide to rain on your parade. The moisture content values in the following table are approximate and can vary depending on the exact material.

After emptying food scraps, use your kitchen collector to add water to a dry compost pile.

MOISTURE CONTENT OF COMMON MATERIALS IN COMPOSTING

Material	Moisture Content (% Net Weight)
Vegetables and fruits	80–90%
Grass clippings	80%
Leaves	40%
Sawdust	40%
Shrub trimmings	15%

Bad Odors and How to Avoid Them

The three most common causes of bad odors in a compost pile are:

1   **Lack of Air (an anaerobic pile):** If the pile doesn't get enough air, the aerobic (air-loving) microorganisms pack their bags and move out while the anaerobic microorganisms set up shop. This is bad for us. Aerobic bacteria decompose material faster and with very little odor. Anaerobic bacteria decompose material slowly and create a rotten-egg smell that will have you wrinkling your nose and stepping backward. Lack of air results if the pile is too wet or too compacted. You can fix this odor by aerating the pile and adding shredded newspaper or dry leaves if the pile is too wet.

2   **Decomposing Food Scraps:** Your compost should never smell like an old garbage can. If it does, bury your food scraps deeper in the pile. A layer of leaves will mask most smells and keep nosy critters away from your bin at the same time. If you have a particularly good sense of smell, you can try adding biochar or activated carbon, which are now much more common in stores. Bury very smelly foods, such as rotten broccoli, deep in the pile.

3   **Too Much Nitrogen:** Sometimes backyard compost piles will start to smell a bit like ammonia (think rotten fish or strong urine). This unpleasant smell results from adding too much high-nitrogen (green) material and not enough carbon-rich (brown) material. You can easily remedy this problem by adding dry leaves or sawdust to your pile.

Harvest the Rain with a Rain Barrel

RAIN BARRELS and composters go together like peanut butter and jelly or Batman and Robin. Oftentimes, people interested in one are also interested in the other. A rain barrel is any large container that you connect to a downspout to collect water falling on your roof during a rainstorm. They range in attractiveness and price, and homeowners often harness the DIY spirit and create their own.

Because the water falling from the sky does not have chlorine, it's ideal for adding moisture to your backyard compost pile. People with rain barrels save this rain to water plants during drier weather. Rain barrels save money by reducing the amount of water you have to pull from the tap to use in your garden.

Streams and other local waterways benefit from your rain barrel as well. During a large storm event, especially in older urban areas, storm sewers and combined sewers become overwhelmed by all the water running off parking lots, buildings, and other impervious surfaces. This blast of water unnaturally surges into the streams, harming wildlife, such as fish and frogs, and tearing up the habitat on the edges. A 1,500-square-foot roof will produce 935 gallons of water during a 1-inch rain event.

One necessary feature to look for when building or buying a rain barrel is a method to connect the overflow from the rain barrel back into the storm sewer. Once you have filled your barrel, you do not want the excess water to flood your basement by pouring onto your foundation. A spigot or spout on the rain barrel that allows you to hook up a hose or fill a watering can is essential. Otherwise, you will have to pull the lid off and dip from the barrel or siphon the water from the top. Some models have a nice area on the top where you can plant plants and even a wick that dips down into the barrel so the plants are self-watering (as long as water remains in the barrel). Consider adding a rain barrel to your list of earth-friendly practices around your home. Before you know it, you'll have solar panels and a green roof too.

This rain barrel's spigot makes it easier to attach a hose for watering.

Compost Activators and Inoculants

Otherwise known as cheater, cheater, pumpkin eaters, compost activators are materials you add to your pile outside of the regular food scraps and yard trimmings to speed up decomposition. Activators generally add a boost of nitrogen, and inoculants generally add beneficial microorganisms especially designed to break down your material.

Prepackaged activators that you buy usually contain bone meal, blood meal, dried manure, and/or enzymes. Luckily, you needn't spend money for good activators. These materials will boost your nitrogen for "free":

Manure (herbivore only)
Coffee grounds
Grass clippings
Old beer and wine
Comfrey

Urine also acts as a nice nitrogen boost if you have any to spare. One activator you may not expect to add to your compost pile that you would have to purchase is dry dog food. Make sure you buy a cheap one with a good amount of some type of meal mixed in. Dog food contains a high amount of nitrogen and will speed up decomposition in your pile.

As for beneficial microorganisms, keep some of your old compost to add to your new pile to help repopulate your microorganism colonies. Adding old compost to your new materials is much like using a starter to make sourdough or Amish friendship bread. Compost activators simply give your pile a little oomph; only add them if you want faster decomposition.

Hot Composting

Think of hot composting as graduate-level composting. Hot composting is a technique governing what you put in and how you maintain compost that is, frankly, a lot of work but results in super-fast finished compost. This method, also referred to as batch composting or active composting, employs every possible advantage to create the optimal environment for microbial activity within a compost pile. That microbial activity generates heat, causing the pile to increase in temperature and rapidly decompose.

People using hot composting techniques, we'll call them hot composters, generate finished compost in as little as three weeks.

Hot Composting Materials

Hot composting requires that you add all your materials at once, rather than over the weeks and months you naturally generate the materials. This means you will need to freeze a month's worth of kitchen scraps, run to your local coffee shop for a donation of used grounds, and stockpile your leaves and yard trimmings until you have enough to make a large pile.

All materials you add to a hot compost pile should be chopped or ground as small as possible. You can't add a whole pumpkin or even a whole stalk of celery. Keeping everything smaller than 2 inches will increase surface area and speed up decomposition. Branches and unchipped wood have no place in a hot compost pile.

You also need to perfectly balance the carbon and nitrogen in your pile. Add three parts brown for every one part green. Traditional composting allows you more variation in brown versus green, but the 3:1 ratio must be perfect for hot composting to really work.

Suggested Hot Compost Recipe:

6 parts dry shredded leaves
3 parts shredded newspaper or straw
1 part manure or coffee grounds
1 part fresh grass clippings or yard trimmings
1 part food scraps (chopped small)
1 shovelful good finished compost

Food scraps and grass clippings will be covered with shredded leaves in this hot compost pile.

Building the Pile

Maintaining a hot composting pile is far easier as a pile on the ground than in a premanufactured bin. You can also use a two- or three-unit system with fronts that easily open. You end up turning the pile very frequently when hot composting, so easy access is critical. The pile needs to measure at least 3 feet by 3 feet.

Start with a layer of straw to improve airflow in the pile. As you build the pile, the easiest way to ensure a good ratio is to add the brown and green materials in thin layers that can easily mix. Halfway up the pile, add a shovelful of old compost or another activator.

Straw can improve airflow in a compost pile and provide a high-carbon balance to food scraps.

Maintaining the Pile

Once built, keep a close eye on the pile to make sure it stays as wet as a wrung-out sponge. The Berkeley Method of hot composting, developed by the University of California–Berkeley, requires you to leave the pile untouched for the first 4 days and then turn every other day for 14 days (turn on day 5, 7, 9, etc.). When you turn a hot compost pile, you remove the outside of the pile first and use that to create the inside of a new pile nearby. You then use the inside of the old pile to create the outside of the new pile.

Hot Composting Schedule (Berkeley Method)

Day 1	Day 2	Day 3	Day 4	Day 5	Day 6	Day 7	Day 8	Day 9
Build Pile	Rest	Rest	Rest	Turn Pile	Rest	Turn Pile	Rest	Turn Pile
Day 10	**Day 11**	**Day 12**	**Day 13**	**Day 14**	**Day 15**	**Day 16**	**Day 17**	**Day 18**
Rest	Turn Pile	Rest	Turn Pile	Rest	Turn Pile	Rest	Turn Pile	Harvest

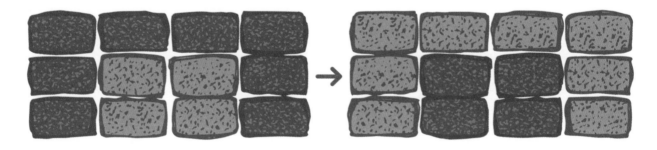

Moving material from the outside of the old pile into the center of the new one provides more evenly decomposed compost.

The pile should maintain a temperature between 131 and 149°F. If you notice a thin layer of white fungus growing, the pile may have exceeded the desired temperature.

Hot composting requires a commitment of time and energy, but if you want compost fast and have the willpower to put in the effort, you may soon call yourself a hot composter.

Winter Compost Maintenance

Anticipating winter gives animals an edge for survival in the wild, and preparing for the impending cold will give you an edge as a successful composter (although natural selection among composters is much less brutal than in the wild). If you live in an area that experiences cold winters, you will need to change a few maintenance habits during the colder months of the year. Much like the rest of us huddling in our homes against the cold weather, happy to hibernate for a few months, life in your compost pile slows down and could go completely dormant. Most of the microorganisms responsible for decomposition cannot withstand freezing temperatures.

Winter composting tips fall into two categories: tips everyone should follow and tips you can choose to follow if you want to be an overachiever.

Tips everyone should follow:

- Harvest your compost in the fall so that you have plenty of room in your bin for a piling up of food scraps.
- Layer in leaves every time you add food scraps. They may not be breaking down much now, but adding a layer of leaves on your food scraps in the winter will stack the deck for the warmer weather. Once spring hits, your pile will be nicely balanced and decompose quickly.
- Do not hand aerate or turn your pile in the winter. Since the pile is mostly dormant, turning it will be a waste of time and may even freeze the last holdout microorganisms huddled in the middle of the pile.

Now for the overachiever tips. You can take extra precautions to prevent your pile from freezing and continue the decomposition over the winter. If you have a hot compost pile, it could be generating enough heat to withstand a mild winter. The secret to keeping your microorganisms munching through the cold is to insulate your compost pile against the elements.

Straw bales, giant piles of leaves, cardboard, and leftover home insulation materials can also be used to surround your compost bin to keep the warm in and the cold out. You can even pile snow as insulation around your compost bin if you live in an area covered by a few feet of snow all winter. Insulate the sides and the top of the bin for the best effect.

The next tip for keeping your compost cooking over the winter is to continue to add food scraps and other high-nitrogen materials. Without fuel, your microbial party will soon putter out. Layer in leaves to keep it balanced and make it easy on your friends by chopping up those food scraps for quick winter snacking.

Overachiever winter composting tips:

- Insulate the sides and top of your bin with straw, leaves, or leftover insulation.
- Continue adding food scraps all winter.
- Chop materials smaller to make decomposition faster.

If you chose to go the lazy route like me and not insulate your bin for the winter, Mother Nature will help your materials decompose with the natural freeze-thaw cycle. Every time it freezes, the water inside your food scraps and wet plant material expands, helping break apart the material's structure. Water expands by about 9 percent from its liquid to solid state. Since food scraps have a high water content (roughly 80 to 90 percent), that means a lot of expansion. After dozens of freeze-thaw cycles, that banana peel is basically "prechewed" and on the fast track for spring bacteria and fungi to finish the job.

TROUBLESHOOTING PROBLEMS WITH YOUR COMPOST BIN

Problem	Cause	Solution
Pile smells garbagy.	Food scraps are exposed or too close to surface.	Bury your food scraps with leaves every time you add food scraps.
Pile has a strong ammonia smell.	Pile has too much nitrogen (green).	Add more carbon (brown) material, such as dry brown leaves, shredded newspaper, or cardboard.
Pile smells like a swamp or rotten eggs.	Pile has too much moisture/water.	Leave the lid off your bin and incorporate dry material until it is as wet as a wrung-out sponge.
Pile is not decomposing.	Pile is either too dry, too small, or needs more nitrogen.	Make sure your pile is as wet as a wrung-out sponge, add more material until your pile is 3′×3′×3′, and add high-nitrogen material such as food scraps.
Pile has lots of sticks or matted leaves.	Material is too large to decompose.	Shred or break apart the material before you place it in the compost pile.
Ants, bees, or some other annoying pests are living in my bin.	Pile is not hot enough to discourage unwanted guests.	Turn the pile and add some high-nitrogen material, such as food scraps or grass clippings.
Plants are growing in my bin.	You either have finished compost that needs harvesting or your pile is not hot enough.	Harvest the finished compost or aerate the pile to encourage it to heat up.

A Quick Way to Get Rid of Fruit Flies

FRUIT FLIES are the tiny but pesky flying insects that seem to appear out of nowhere to swarm your kitchen collector and compost bin, especially during the summer. These little buggers actually ride into your home on your produce as larvae or eggs (just another reason to wash that apple before you eat it). Aside from pulling out a miniature fly swatter, you can take a few easy steps to discourage or reduce their nuisance.

If a swarm of fruit flies seems to attack you when you lift the lid of your compost bin, you need to bury your food scraps. These small insects will not burrow down into a pile to lay their eggs on your food scraps. If you cover the scraps with leaves, the flies will venture elsewhere.

Occasionally, these flies appear in your kitchen (don't worry, they bother non-composters too), but you can take preventative action here as well.

Ideas for discouraging fruit flies in your kitchen:

- Take out your kitchen scraps daily or several times a day when flies are in your kitchen.
- Cover food scraps added to your kitchen collector with sawdust.
- Use a kitchen collector with a tight-fitting lid.
- Create a fruit-fly trap.

You can create a simple fruit-fly trap with a small plastic container with a clear lid. Poke several holes in the clear lid. Place a banana peel and some apple cider vinegar in the container, replace the lid, and set the container in an area where the flies congregate. The sweet smells from the apple cider vinegar and banana peel will draw the flies in through the holes, but they will not be able to escape. If the plight of the poor imprisoned flies pulls at your heartstrings, you can release them into the wild (a.k.a. your backyard)—just stay away from your compost bin.

BACKYARD COMPOST MAINTENANCE CALENDAR*

Spring	Summer	Fall	Winter
Gather remaining brown leaves in your yard to add to the pile.	Bury food scraps under leaves.	Gather falling leaves for compost. Construct extra leaf bins or piles if needed.	The pile goes dormant.
Aerate compost at least monthly.	Aerate compost at least monthly.	Aerate compost at least monthly.	Do not aerate or turn.
Harvest in late spring if you need compost for starting seeds or new beds.	Find alternative sources of carbon-rich brown material if your leaves run out. Shredded newspaper or cardboard work well.	Harvest compost to make room for the buildup of winter materials.	Continue adding food scraps and burying them under leaves.
Ensure that spring rains do not overwater the compost pile.	Water the pile if hot weather dries it out.	Add old plant trimmings to the pile.	Insulate the pile if you desire an active pile throughout the winter.
Add spring weeds, old potting soil, and last year's plants to the pile.	Grasscycle (see Chapter 6) when possible, or add your cut grass to your compost.	Visit your local coffee shop and ask for their spent coffee grounds to incorporate into your leaf piles.	Chop material into smaller pieces to allow for easier decomposition.
Start a hot composting pile if you need finished compost in a hurry.	Turn or mix materials in the pile at least once over the summer.	Consider not adding food scraps for a few weeks before harvesting compost. Place them in the freezer and add them to your bin after harvest.	Enjoy a nice mug of hot cocoa by the fire and relax.

*Your maintenance schedule may vary depending on your area's climate and the type of composting system you have. This calendar follows the maintenance required for a typical backyard compost bin in a temperate climate.

5

IN-VESSEL COMPOSTING TECHNIQUES

CHOOSING A COMPOSTING STYLE

Composting is much like cooking soup. You can make soup thousands of different ways using many different recipes and end up with unique yet delicious results each time. In the same way, no two compost piles are identical, yet each will yield a beneficial amendment for your soil. Backyard composters have harnessed human ingenuity to produce numerous creative variations. Let's break down the different styles so that you can decide what is right for you and your home.

COMPOSTING STYLES

A bin contains your food scraps and yard trimmings while they turn into compost.

Of course, with so much human ingenuity, we are bound to end up with techniques that do not fall neatly into single categories. The garbage-can composter described later in this chapter fits this description. Part "food digester" and part composter, it uses a unique buried method to secure the bin against furry critters while decomposing food scraps. Other composting methods, such as trench composting and African keyhole gardens, incorporate aspects of your garden to help fertilize your plants where they live. We will discuss these types of integrated composting in Chapter 6. Consider looking at the "Which Composting Method Is Right for You?" flowchart at the end of the book to help chose a method that fits your lifestyle and home.

This chapter delves into in-vessel composting, or composting in some type of container. From the very basic leaf bin to the serious gardener system, we will walk through many different methods and step-by-step instructions to help you to create your own custom composting oasis.

Wire Leaf Bin

Wire bins take the award for the easiest type of bin to build. One step up from just piling material on the ground, they manage to keep leaves and yard trimmings in a nice contained area while not looking obtrusive next to landscaping. Wire bins and their counterparts make fantastic vessels for holding the large amount of leaves dumped on us each year. By containing the leaves and yard trimmings in a certain area, you speed up decomposition and help maintain a tidier yard.

Leaf bins come premade in the store or online in both metal and plastic. You can use almost any type of wire fencing or even plastic fencing to build these types of bins yourself. You can also choose any type of fastener to hold the bin in place. Metal wire, carabiners, or even garbage twist ties will do the trick in a pinch.

A word of caution: Leaf bins do not make great places to compost food scraps. Squirrels, raccoons, mice, and even deer can usually find a way to munch on your leftovers. If you don't want to feed the local wildlife, stick with adding leaves and yard trimmings to a wire bin. You can try burying food scraps in a few feet of leaves to make the bin less tempting, but animals are accustomed to foraging for food. Adding food scraps to a wire bin basically creates a critter buffet garnished with leaves.

How to Speed Up Leaf Composting

Leaves are the key ingredient in most backyard composting.

LEAVES will obviously decompose without your assistance, but depending on the species, the process may take several years. With a few tricks, you can turn fall leaves into spring compost. First, shred the leaves. This may require running over them with a lawnmower or going at them with a weed trimmer. If you want an afternoon of real fun, buy or rent a leaf mulcher, which acts like a small chipper shredder but only for leaves. Once the leaves are smaller, the macro- and microorganisms can break them down much faster.

NEXT, add a high-nitrogen material, preferably coffee grounds. Most animals dislike the smell of coffee grounds, so you won't attract unwanted guests as you would with other food scraps, but you will receive the benefit of the nitrogen to help break down the high-carbon leaves. Layering the coffee grounds in the leaves as you pile them up is more effective than just throwing the coffee grounds on top. Many local coffee shops will gladly share their spent coffee grounds with gardeners and composters, so you can access bulk grounds without brewing enough coffee for an army.

One last tip: Add urine to the leaf pile. Urine is high in available liquid nitrogen and acts immediately to help decompose the leaves. Of course, use discretion in how the urine gets to the pile. Direct application may result in a few raised eyebrows from onlooking neighbors.

Partially composted leaves make a great free mulch in your garden.

DIY WIRE LEAF BIN

Building a leaf bin is easy peasy. It will probably take you more time to gather the supplies than to actually construct the bin. Depending on the annual bounty of leaves you expect in your yard, you may want to build multiple structures or a larger bin. A 3-foot-tall leaf bin with a 3-foot diameter will hold the same amount of leaves as five paper leaf bags. A 3-foot-tall leaf bin with a 4-foot diameter will hold the same amount of leaves as nine paper leaf bags.

Leaves will settle quickly in a leaf bin, usually shrinking to half their original volume in just a month or two. With any luck, a full leaf bin will make room for more leaves before the next time you have to rake.

The following instructions are for building a 3-foot-diameter bin. For a 4-foot-diameter bin, you'll need 12½ feet of wire fencing, but the basic steps remain the same.

This simple wire compost bin holds leaves, grass clippings, and plants trimmed from the garden.

Materials Needed:

1 10' wire fencing, 3' tall
2 Aviation shears
3 Zip ties
4 Gloves
5 Safety glasses
6 Tape measure

Suggested Simple Wire Leaf Bin Recipe:

10 parts shredded leaves

1 part coffee grounds

Let's Do It ➜

1
Measure out 10' of wire fencing. Galvanized steel is easy to work with and stays sturdy and straight in the backyard.

2
Use wire cutters to cut the fencing as near the intersections as possible so that little metal spikes don't snag your clothes or skin. Wear gloves and cut carefully, as this metal can be sharp.

3
Form the wire fencing into a circle 3' in diameter. The fencing will overlap and add strength to the final bin.

4
Use zip ties to secure the overlapping fencing to itself.

5
Place the bin where you want it and fill it up with leaves.

To harvest a leaf bin, simply lift the bin off the leaves and scoop up your gorgeous compost. Soil scientists and gardeners refer to finished compost made mostly of leaves as "leaf mold." Although leaf mold does not have the high values of nitrogen and other nutrients that traditional compost contains, it has a fantastic texture that helps amend soils and improve water retention for your plants.

Contained Single-Unit Bin

Many people who compost fall into the broad category of single-unit composters. Store-bought black plastic bins range from roughly square boxes to the cylindrical "Darth Vader helmet" styles, but all work quite well. These types of units have no bottom to allow worms and other useful decomposers open access to your pile but are secure everywhere else to keep out raccoons, mice, squirrels, and their buddies. They hold in heat and moisture to speed decomposition, and their compact size fits nicely into even tiny backyards.

Although great bins for composting food scraps, yard trimmings, and leaves, single-unit composting becomes inadequate if you are blessed with a tree-heavy yard. You may need to make an additional bin just for leaves. Many composters choose to have two or even three traditional compost bins so they have one "cooking" while the other is filling.

You can create single-unit bins out of pallets, cement blocks, or any scrap materials you have that fasten together to make a box with an open bottom and an optional lid.

DIY CONVERTED TRASH CAN COMPOSTER

Many of us already have the makings of this unique composter lying around at home. The original concept was presented in *Mother Earth News* in 1976 and differs from other compost bins that simply rest on top of the ground. This composter goes subterranean by living in a 15-inch-deep hole surrounded by soil. Holes drilled around the lower sides and in the bottom of the can allow water to seep out and worms and other organisms to creep in. The secure lid keeps out unwanted critters.

You can make this bin with either plastic or metal, but your Oscar the Grouch impersonation during construction will be much more believable with the metal bin.

Materials Needed:

1 Galvanized metal trash can with lid
2 Drill
3 Drill bit, at least ¼"
4 Shovel
5 Gloves
6 Safety glasses

Let's Do It ➔

1

Turn the can upside down and drill 20 to 30 holes in the bottom of the can. This process creates metal shards, which you can easily wipe away.

2

Drill 20 to 30 holes around the bottom sides of the can. Go about 15" up the can. The higher you go, the deeper the hole you have to dig.

3

Choose a well-drained spot in your yard to dig the hole. Use the can to imprint the ground, giving you a guide to the needed width of the hole.

4

Dig the hole. You can periodically dip the can into the hole to see how much deeper you need to go.

5
Once you have reached your desired depth, place the can into the hole and fill around the outside with soil.

6
Place a shallow layer of wood chips or straw in the bottom of the can to improve drainage.

7
Add your food scraps and cover them with leaves. Secure the lid. If you have especially persistent critter neighbors, you could secure the lid further with a bungee cord across the top hooked onto the handles.

Garbage-can composters need aeration just like other types of bins. The easiest tool to use in the tight space is the hand aerator (see Chapter 3). If you suspend adding food scraps for about a month before you harvest, you will have less work pulling out a nice batch of compost. Simply lift the can out of the ground (this may require two people) and empty it where you want to use the finished compost. Screen it into a wheelbarrow if you desire a finer finished compost.

Suggested Garbage Can Composter Recipe

1 shovelful mulch, wood chips, or straw

3 parts shredded leaves

1 part food scraps

Always Bury Food Scraps

FOOD SCRAPS—such as banana peels, old broccoli, and stale bread—are a fantastic source of nitrogen to complement the dry, carbon-rich leaves in your compost. Readily available in every kitchen and with little other use (unless you own chickens), food scraps also add water and additional microorganisms to your compost. The most important step in adding food scraps to your compost is to bury your food scraps.

Let me say that again: Bury your food scraps!

As they decompose, food scraps can start to smell garbagy and attract critters to the bin. They also attract flies that will lay eggs and create pesky swarms every time you lift the lid. To avoid odors, animals, and flies, all you have to do is bury your food scraps in your pile or cover them with leaves.

You can effectively bury your food scraps by having a pile of leaves set aside for the sole purpose of throwing in after you deposit food scraps. Alternatively, use a hand trowel to lift up a layer in the pile and tuck your food scraps under a blanket of leaves and other compost. Either way, you should not be able to see the food scraps once buried. Fruit flies will not burrow down into the leaves to lay eggs, and the leaves will act as a scent barrier to foraging animals.

Contained Two- or Three-Unit Bin

All serious gardeners acknowledge the undeniable benefit of compost, and most maintain their own compost-bin system. If you want to join their ranks, you need a system that can handle a larger volume of material and allows easy access to finished compost. Serious gardeners tend to have more material from clipping plants and weeding, but they also tend to seek out compost fodder from outside sources. They grab extra coffee grounds from the local coffee shop and happily accept bags of their neighbors' leaves.

Having a multiple-bin system allows gardeners to move material from the first bin into the second before filling the first bin again. This movement provides air to the compost and speeds decomposition, something very important to gardeners who not only have a large amount of material to handle but also clamor for the finished compost to use in their gardens.

You can set up multiple smaller bins or opt to build your own compost system. Whether from wood and wire or reused pallets (a.k.a. skids), these compost structures are worth the extra effort in the long run.

DIY WOOD AND WIRE TWO-BIN COMPOSTER

Possibly tying with the tumbler for fanciest and certainly the favorite of serious gardeners, the wood and wire bin offers great airflow, great capacity, and a good amount of critter-proof security. I may be biased, but I also think this type of bin looks natural in the garden.

This may seem like an intimidating list of materials (and if you have never used power tools, you probably should not start with this project), but you can make this bin in a weekend with generous time for breaks.

Constructed as described, you will have the Cadillac of compost bins, but you could easily adapt this into a two-bin unit made out of wood pallets or other lumber. Cedar is naturally weather- and pest-resistant and smells *amazing* when you cut into the board. Grade A cedar boards or pressure-treated lumber would use the dimensions listed below. Using rough-sawn cedar from a specialty lumber yard will save a considerable amount of money (it'd be about half the cost), but the boards come in a larger size than dimensional lumber (the smooth variety). With a little extra math, you can make rough-sawn cedar work.

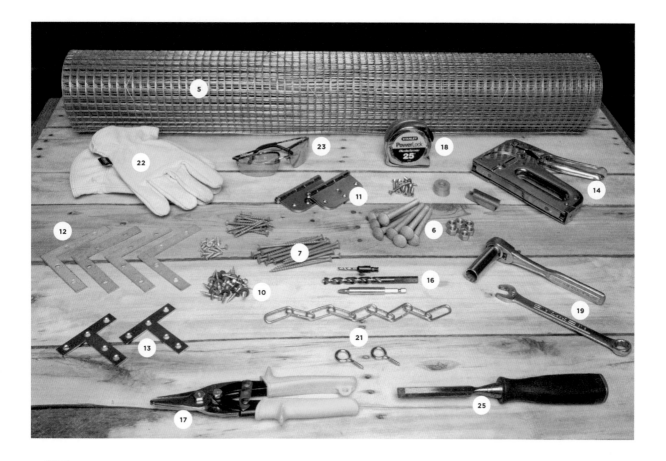

Materials Needed:

1 *2 × 4 cedar boards, (6) 31½", (6) 36",*
(4) 6', (3) 29"
2 *2 × 2 cedar boards, (4) 34½", (1) 6', (3) 29"*
3 *2 × 6 cedar boards, (3) 36"*
4 *1 × 6 cedar boards, (12) 31"*
5 21' (¼") hardware cloth, 36" wide
6 Carriage bolts, (8) 3½" × ⅜" with
washers and nuts
7 3½" wood decking screws, a 1-lb. box
8 *Corrugated roofing, (3) 32" × 26" pieces*
9 *Wiggle molding, 12'*
10 Gasketed roofing screws (40)
11 Hinges, (2) galvanized or stainless
12 Galvanized flat corner braces, (4) 4"

13 Galvanized flat T-braces, (2) 4"
14 Staple gun and staples (⅜" or similar)
15 *Drill*
16 Drill bits
17 Aviation shears
18 Tape measure
19 ¾" socket or box wrench or
adjustable wrench
20 *Carpenter's square*
21 Hook eyes (2) and 8" of chain
22 Gloves
23 Safety glasses
24 *Ear protection*
25 Wood chisel

 Pictured    *Not shown*

Let's Do It ➜

Building the Main Structure

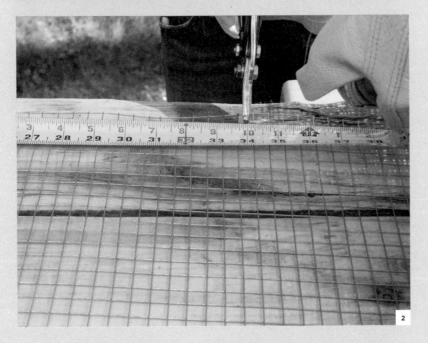

1

Screw together two 31½" 2 × 4s
and two 36" 2 × 4s with wood
decking screws to create a
rectangle. The two 36" pieces
sandwich the smaller boards. Do
this three times, forming the two
ends and the center divider. If you
predrill the holes before screwing,
the wood is less likely to split.
Make these boxes as square as
possible or your finished compost
bin will set a bit wonky.

2

Wearing gloves, cut three 33½"
hardware cloth pieces (33½" × 36").
Cut as close to the wire intersections
as possible to avoid snags. After
cutting each piece, cut the orphan
ends to start with a fresh edge.

3

Staple the hardware cloth to the frames. It helps to have a two-person system so one person can hold the cloth tight while the other staples. Starting in the middle of a board will also help keep the pieces straight. Remember, staples cost only $3 for 1,000, so you can afford to be a bit generous to make sure the mesh is secure.

4

Now attach the three 6' 2 × 4s to the three frames you just assembled. Drill a ⅜" hole at each intersection and install the carriage bolts to attach the frames to the 6' 2 × 4s. Ensure the hardware cloth faces out for the two outside frames. If you want to skip the carriage bolts, you could do this with deck carpentry screws, but carriage bolts offer a tight fit and a stronger hold. The upper front does not have a 2 × 4 for easier turning.

5
The bottom of the bin has gaps between the two 6' 2 × 4s. Screw 29" 2 × 4s onto the bottom of the frames to fill in the gaps. These gap-fillers act only as a surface for the hardware cloth, so you can assemble them with multiple scrap pieces if needed.

6
Wearing gloves, cut two 6' pieces of hardware cloth (6' × 36"). Staple these pieces on the back and the bottom of the bin. It is easiest to start in the middle, followed by the corners, and then fill in the areas in between with staples. The bottom does not have to have the hardware cloth, but it will keep digging critters, such as moles, out of your bin. Feel free to skip the mesh on the bottom if you wish.

Constructing the Lid

1

Assemble the lid with three 29″ 2 × 2s for the side and center brace pieces, one 6′ 2 × 2 for the front brace, and one 6′ 2 × 4 for the back brace (for extra support). The long pieces sandwich the shorter pieces. You will use the metal flat corner braces and flat T-braces for this task. If you are looking to add some strength training to your life, you could make this lid out of all 2 × 4s, but the result is very heavy.

2

Cut the corrugated roofing into three 32″ pieces with tin snips.

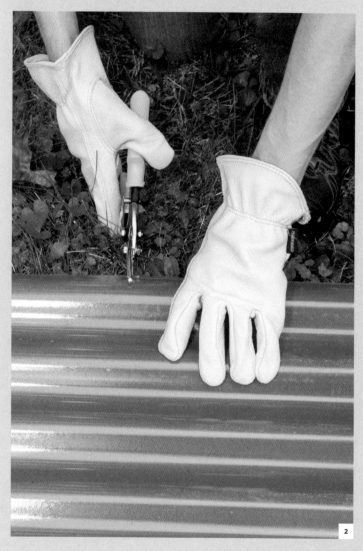

3

Leaving room on the back board for the hinge, place the wiggle molding along the front and back edges of the lid. Wiggle molding easily snaps together to form a 6' piece.

4

Place roofing pieces on the wiggle molding. If your roofing has a glossy side, put that side up. Make sure each piece overlaps by about 1". Drive the screws into the bottom of the divot through the wiggle molding and into the board.

5

Set the lid on the main structure and attach the hinges. Practice opening and shutting the lid to make sure you leave enough room for the hinges.

6

Attach eye hooks to the edge of the lid and the main bin. Connect with a chain to prevent the lid from falling backward.

Creating the Front Slats

1

Screw three 36" 2 × 6 boards to the front of the frame. Closing the lid on the compost bin will help you gauge where the slats should go.

2

To create the track into which the slats will slide, screw the four 34½" 2 × 2s on the inside of the frame. You want to leave enough room for the boards to easily slide up and down.

3

At this point, test the 1 × 6 slats in the track and cut off any length necessary to help the boards fit easily. You may also chisel the frame to create a smoother slide. Spending a little extra time on this step now will save you frustration later when you want to turn the pile.

Once you slide the slats into place, your bin is complete. Start by filling one of the units with leaves, yard trimmings, and food scraps. After a few months or when the first unit is full, slide out the slats and use a pitchfork to move everything into the second unit. This adds air to the composting material. By the time you have filled the first unit again, you will probably have finished compost in the second.

The two-unit wire and mesh bin was adapted from designs created by Andrew Sigal and StopWaste.org.

Suggested Two-Unit Composter Recipe

6 parts shredded leaves

1 part food scraps or coffee grounds

1 part plant trimmings

Keeping Animals Out of Your Compost

ONE MAJOR FACTOR to consider when choosing a composting technique is how you will keep animals, especially rodents, out of your compost pile. In an urban environment, rodents such as rats and mice prove to have very sharp teeth and a particularly determined mindset when it comes to accessing your rotting fruits and vegetables.

Aside from burying your food scraps in leaves and using coffee grounds, you can also sprinkle cayenne pepper on top of the bin to deter them. Perhaps the best defense against rodents is choosing a very hardy compost bin to keep them out. If you build the two-bin unit in an urban setting, use ¼- to ½-inch wire mesh with 16- to 20-gauge strength. With strong wire and wood and a sturdy, secure lid, this bin may more effectively keep out rats than even a plastic bin, as rats have been known to chew through plastic bins.

The buried trash can made of galvanized metal also offers good rodent protection, and the tumbler has a nice secure lid and offers quick disposal of food scraps. Should you encounter digging rodents, secure some wire mesh underneath your bin, which will effectively act as a composting bouncer—our soil friends can get through, but the rodents can't. If you design your own bin, ensure that it has no openings greater than ¼ inch.

Tumbler

The Grateful Dead of composters, tumblers have a loyal and dedicated following. These bins are up off the ground in some barrel-type contraption that either spins or rolls to add air to the compost. Tumblers will make finished compost fast if you know how to maintain them.

Composting in a tumbler is a bit more hands-on than other methods. You will need to consider the following:

1. Balancing the greens and browns you add.
2. Assessing the level of moisture.
3. Adding beneficial microorganisms.

Tumblers have the advantage of being easy to turn, which means you will add air more often than with a traditional compost bin. Adding that air helps activate the good bacteria and heat up the compost material quickly. Some composters claim to harvest finished compost in just a few weeks with their tumbler.

The biggest mistake composters make when using tumblers is adding too many food scraps and not enough brown material. Food scraps will turn into a sloshy, stinky mess without the balance of the dry brown material.

You also need to carefully monitor the moisture level with tumblers. Composters on the ground have the advantage of easily draining into the soil if too much moisture builds up. Even tumblers with drain holes can accumulate too much water (again—sloshy, stinky mess). If you squeeze your compost (gloves on, remember) and you can squeeze out a significant amount of water, it is too wet and needs shredded paper or leaves immediately.

Because tumblers exist suspended off the soil, they do not benefit from migrating microorganisms as a traditional bin does. You can remedy this situation by adding a few shovelfuls of good living soil from your yard or by purchasing beneficial microorganisms. After your first batch, keep a little of the old compost behind to inoculate the new material.

Tumblers also require that you stop adding materials to the bin about 3 weeks before you plan to harvest. Tumblers work best using batch composting. You wouldn't pull cookies out of the oven halfway through baking to add more flour, so don't add more food scraps while your tumbler finishes the compost decomposition. Freeze the food scraps in the meantime until you are ready to start a new batch.

DIY COMPOST TUMBLER

You can purchase premade tumblers for a pretty penny, or you can use the following instructions to make your own. This model reuses an old pickle barrel sourced from a local pickle company for $20. Why buy new when you can give something a second life?

The vent tube in the middle will bring air into the compost and help reduce the sloshy, messy issues of some tumblers. If your store does not carry the threaded galvanized pipe in the right size, ask if they can custom-cut and thread it for you. Metal window screens are the perfect type of wire mesh to keep the air vent free of insects, such as bees, that may want to call your compost tumbler home. You could forgo the stand and just roll the barrel around on the ground, but the stand does add a level of class to the project (yes, this is a classy pickle barrel).

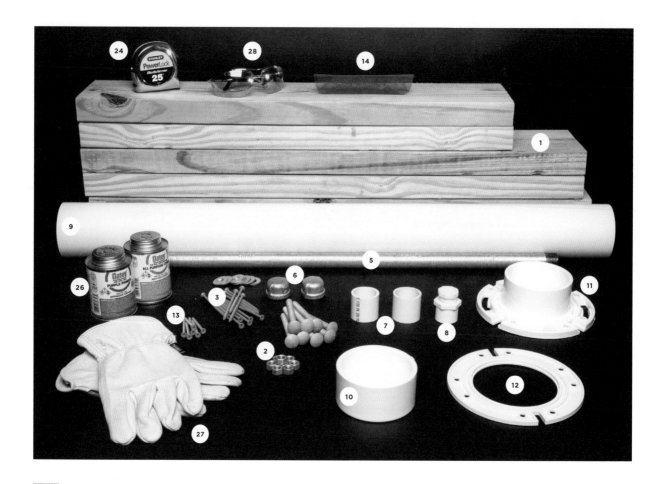

Materials Needed:

1 2 × 6 treated lumber boards, (4) 33½", (2) 28½"
2 Carriage bolts, (8) 3½" × ⅜" with washers and nuts
3 3½" wood decking screws, (12)
4 *60-gallon food-grade plastic barrel*
5 ¾" galvanized pipe nipple, threaded on both ends, 30" long
6 ¾" galvanized threaded pipe cap (2)
7 1¼" PVC pipe, (2) 1½" long
8 ¾" schedule 40 PVC plug
9 3" schedule 40 PVC pipe, 36" long
10 3" schedule 40 PVC cap
11 3" schedule 40 PVC closet flange
12 3" schedule 40 PVC closet flange spacer ring
13 #7 self-tapping screws, (4) 2"

14 Wire mesh (used for screen doors)
15 *Wire cutters*
16 *Drill and drill bits*
17 *1¼" hole saw*
18 *Jigsaw*
19 *Compound miter saw*
20 *Channel-type pliers*
21 *Adjustable wrench or socket set*
22 *Razor knife or utility knife*
23 *Screwdriver*
24 Tape measure
25 *Hammer*
26 PVC cement
27 Gloves
28 Safety glasses

 Pictured   *Not shown*

DIY COMPOST TUMBLER

Let's Do It →

Prepare the Barrel

1

On the bottom of the barrel, mark the opening for the flange. Use the barrel's seam to center the hole. Simply place the bottom (smaller) part of the flange on the barrel and trace your circle.

2

Use a drill to make a hole in the middle big enough to insert your jigsaw blade.

3

Insert the jigsaw blade into the hole and cut a path toward the traced circle. Follow the traced circle to cut out the flange opening.

4 Measure 21½″ up from the bottom of the barrel and drill 1″ holes on opposite sides of the barrel for the axle to pass through. Use the barrel seams to center the holes on each side.

5 To create a drain hole, drill a small 1″ hole in the lowest rim of the barrel.

6 Using a ⅟₁₆″ drill bit, drill very small holes in the plug to make a drain.

7 Thread the plug snugly into the hole in the barrel.

Construct the Frame

1

Cut four 33½" and two 28½" pressure-treated 2 × 6 boards using the compound miter saw. You may save time by asking your local lumberyard to cut these for you.

2

Measure 4 inches down on two of the 33½" 2 × 6 boards and drill a 1" hole centered in each board. These boards will act as the upright supports of the frame.

3

Form a *T* with an upright support and a base piece (33½″ 2 × 6). Drill four evenly spaced holes and join the two pieces using four carriage bolts, nuts, and washers. Make sure the base piece is on the outside with the carriage bolt heads on the outside and the nuts and washers on the inside. Repeat this process with the other upright support and base piece.

4

Attach the center braces (28½″ 2 × 6) on either side of the center supports at the bottom using three 3½″ deck screws at each end (12 total).

5

Cut two small pieces of 1¼″ PVC pipe to 1½″ long. You can use most types of saws for this job. These little pieces of PVC will act as spacers on the axle between the barrel and the frame.

Create an Air Vent

1 First make the air holes for the vent. Drill four rows of evenly spaced ⅜" holes in the 36" PVC pipe. Stagger the holes 1½" apart spanning the length of the long PVC pipe. This work will create PVC shavings, which you can clean away with a razor knife or utility knife. Press the flange into the 36" PVC pipe without glue. Insert the unglued flange and pipe (air vent) into the barrel.

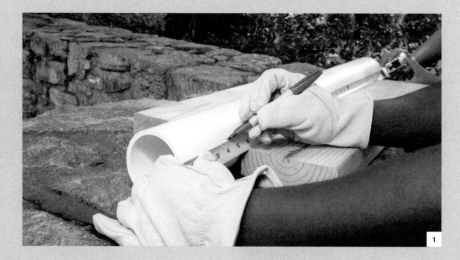

2 Insert the ¾" galvanized pipe (axle) into the barrel and, reaching into the top of the barrel, mark where the galvanized pipe hits the PVC. Repeat marking the pipe on the other side.

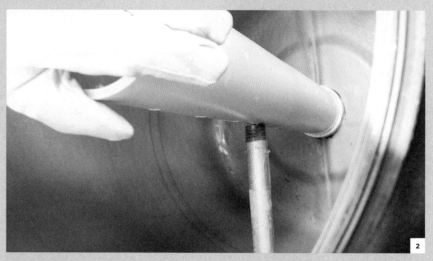

3 Remove the air vent and use a 1" hole saw to cut the holes in the PVC pipe where marked.

4 Use the larger side of the flange as a guide to cut the wire mesh into a circle the size of the widest part of the flange.

Assemble the Tumbler

1

This section is easiest with two people. Screw the cap onto one end of your 30" galvanized pipe nipple (axle). Insert the uncapped end of the axle into one hole of the stand.

2

Slide on the PVC spacer between the stand and the barrel.

3

Have one person hold the barrel and the other person push the galvanized pipe into the first side of the barrel.

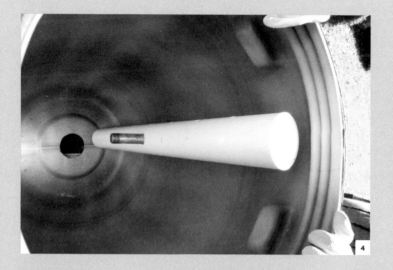

4

Remove the flange from the air vent pipe and insert the pipe into the barrel. Push the galvanized pipe through the recently drilled holes of the air vent. Continue pushing the galvanized pipe through the barrel and out the other side.

5

Install the other small PVC spacer. Push the axle through the other end of the stand and screw the galvanized pipe cap on the other side. Use a hammer to coax it through if the axle gives you any trouble.

6

Flip the barrel upside down and use the PVC cement to glue the flange to the pipe. Immediately fasten the flange tightly to the bottom of the barrel using two 2" self-tapping screws.

7

Sandwich the wire mesh between the flange and flange spacer. Screw 2″ self-tapping screws through the flange and the spacer into the barrel.

8

Place the PVC cap on the other end of the air vent. Leaving this piece unglued will allow you to clean out any small pieces of compost that enter through the air holes.

9

Give the wood a few weeks to dry out, and stain it if you want to gussy up the tumbler. Once the glue sets, you can start filling the tumbler with food scraps and shredded leaves. If the mix gets too wet, try adding shredded cardboard or paper to soak up the excess water. Turn the barrel as frequently as you like, but make sure to turn it at least once per week.

DIY Tumbler design adapted from plans created by C. Peters at www.dixiegrilling.com.

Reuse Rocks

Suggested Tumbler Composting Recipe

2 parts finely shredded leaves
1 part shredded newspaper or cardboard
1 part food scraps
1 part weeds
1 shovelful good garden soil

INTENTIONALLY reusing the products and packaging associated with our everyday lives not only appeals to the frugal, penny-pinching aspect of our personalities but also to our inner environmentalists. In the 3R hierarchy you may have learned about in elementary schools—reduce, reuse, recycle—reuse ranks higher than recycling as having a stronger environmental impact because it uses fewer resources. Composting technically falls into the "recycling" definition since we (or, rather, our microbe friends) transform one material into something new.

Composters have the opportunity to perform a double-duty, earth-friendly act by reusing materials to create an area or vessel for our composting. Reuse and recycling work hand in hand when composting, surely while singing "All You Need Is Love" and flashing peace signs.

You can jump on the reuse bandwagon in multiple ways. Consider shopping for your lumber and other supplies at a building materials reuse center. These are like thrift stores for building supplies, and you can have a lot of fun just walking through the place and discovering treasures. You will generally save 25 to 75 percent off retail prices at a traditional hardware store or lumberyard. Be sure to ask if they allow price negotiation—if they do, you can wind up saving even more money.

Reuse surplus materials you have lying around your house and garage to construct the bins and tools listed in this book. Several projects, such as the screener, offer enough flexibility to use scrap lumber. Instead of purchasing a fancy new kitchen collector, just use an old butter tub or coffee canister. Give the item a facelift by printing a list of what you can compost on a durable sticker for the outside. One frugal gardener designed the DIY auger in Chapter 4 based on supplies she had lying around.

You can also get creative in the sourcing of your supplies. A friend of mine found the used pickle barrel we used to make the tumbler on page 109 far cheaper than you would find a new one online. It even smelled like mouth-watering pickles. Sometimes manufacturers and stores have leftover pallets or skids that make excellent sides for a compost bin.

Many communities have tool rental stores or tool sharing co-ops that allow you to borrow a tool and then return it when you have finished. Borrowing tools or equipment means you do not have to find a place to store it long term and you are not responsible for maintaining the tools or putting out the large up-front cost. How often do you really use that grass aerator or that chipper shredder? How many hours a day does that tool just sit in your shed or garage unused? Imagine how many fewer resources we would use to make the tools we need if everyone in the community shared tools. To slightly modify the lyrics of John Lennon, all we are saying is give reuse a chance.

Bokashi

If you are into brewing your own beer or canning your own vegetables, Bokashi might spark your interest. A Japanese method of fermenting food scraps indoors, Bokashi is more precomposting than full-cycle composting, as you have to finish composting the fermented food scraps in a backyard compost bin or by digging them into the soil. The benefits of holding food scraps in your kitchen for weeks with little odor and creating faster decomposition than traditional methods makes Bokashi worthy of consideration even if it is still a fringe composting practice in the United States.

Bokashi uses controlled anaerobic decomposition by carefully introducing the food scraps to feed beneficial microorganisms that love an anaerobic environment. Bokashi requires two things: a special bucket and inoculated bran. Although I am usually an advocate of DIY, I recommend you buy a special Bokashi bucket and the premade inoculated bran if you want to try this method. The easy-to-use spigot will save you time and give you a higher chance of success.

Start your Bokashi by placing food scraps in the bucket, pressing the air out of them (a dinner plate works well for this purpose), and then sprinkling the food scraps with inoculated bran. After each addition of food scraps and bran, make sure to close the lid. Unlike all other forms of composting, air is the enemy with Bokashi. Every few days, you have to draw off the leachate (the liquid created from composting) using the spigot. The leachate and food scraps in the bucket should smell a little sour and sweet, like fermenting vegetables. Since you control the microorganisms, you should not have the foul odors associated with natural anaerobic decomposition.

After a few weeks, the food scraps still look recognizable, but they have fundamentally changed. The material is now pickled and called "precompost." You can either dig the fermented food scraps into your garden soil or bury them in your traditional backyard compost bin. If you choose the digging into the garden route, do not plant anything on top of the area for at least a few weeks. The material needs to finish decomposing and is still too acidic to come into contact with plant roots.

If you chose the bin route, know that the fermented food scraps are acidic and may slightly alter the pH of your bin. You could add wood ash or another basic material to help counteract the acidity. Also, make sure to bury the food scraps, just as you would the fresh variety, under a nice layer of leaves. These fermented food scraps break down faster than fresh food scraps added to your backyard bin.

Once you experience a few rounds of success with Bokashi, you can start building your own custom Bokashi buckets and inoculating your own bran (or other grain) with the special yeasts and bacteria. If the bran does not work or the food scraps have too much air, Bokashi can transform into a rather disgusting mess that will turn the stomach of even the stoutest person. Bokashi is not for everyone, but if you believe the benefits outweigh the risks, buy the professional kit and give Bokashi a chance. You may help push this fringe practice into mainstream composting.

This inoculated bran controls which microorganisms populate your Bokashi bin.

ADVANTAGES AND DISADVANTAGES OF IN-VESSEL COMPOSTING METHODS

Composting Method	Advantages	Disadvantages
Wire leaf bin	Inexpensive Easy to make Holds many leaves Open to ground Easy harvesting	Does not keep out animals seeking food scraps
Contained single-unit bin	Holds in moisture and heat Secure against animals Open to ground	Limited capacity More complicated harvesting
Contained multi-unit bin	Lots of capacity Open to ground Easier harvesting Can secure against animals	More expensive Need space in yard
Tumbler	Easy to aerate Easy to harvest Secure against animals Fastest finished compost	Not open to ground Need to add microorganisms More expensive Limited capacity
Bokashi	Stays inside home, backyard not needed Requires less space than traditional composting Faster decomposition Secure against animals	Need to finish composting outdoors or in the soil Have to purchase or make bran Less forgiving than traditional composting

6

INTEGRATED COMPOSTING

THINKING OUTSIDE OF THE BIN

Many urban and suburban composters choose to compost in a contained bin since it offers the benefits of holding all your organics in a nice controlled package. However, if you have a little more space or some creativity, you can choose to integrate your composting efforts into your garden or landscaping. Once you escape the confines of your bin, you are free to compost as much material as you want. Let's check out a few tried-and-true techniques.

Simple Compost Pile

Composting needn't be technologically advanced. You can actually throw materials into a pile or heap and they will decompose into finished compost with little or no assistance. Most often we see this method used with leaves or when someone has a very large backyard. One luxury of owning several acres of land is the ease of hiding your compost pile in an unobtrusive spot.

Simple compost piles offer more than one advantage. They are free to start, can expand when the season demands, and are a breeze to turn. Worms and other composting friends have an open invitation to visit, and compost piles tend to drain easily if in the right spot. A word of caution with compost piles: If you add food scraps to an open pile, you are inviting furry four-legged critters over for dinner. Some people enjoy watching rascally raccoons make away with watermelon rinds and carelessly litter corncobs across the yard. While entertaining, you can avoid unwanted visitors by not adding food scraps to an open pile.

We will skip the "Let's Do It" section for the simple compost pile. Seriously, just pile stuff up. Let it rot. Done.

Pit or Trench Composting

Many people living in a homeowner's association or community that prohibits composting choose this method for composting on the down-low. Burying your food scraps under the ground keeps aboveground critters out of your pile while bringing the food scraps to the worms' front door. This technique also hides the evidence and masks all odors associated with decomposing scraps. As an added bonus, once everything you bury decomposes into compost, the material is already integrated into your garden—no need to harvest compost or work the material into the soil.

Underground composting will likely go anaerobic at some point. As anyone who has had the nightmare of being buried alive knows, the air will eventually run out. Because the material is underground, however, you only need to pile a good layer of soil on top and have patience. The soil will mask odors, and given enough time, your material will decompose.

The best places to integrate underground composting are rows in a vegetable garden or a landscaping bed you want to replenish for next year. Pit and trench composting improve soil with little humus material, such as heavy clay or sandy soil, and add nutrients and improve soil structure right in the root zone of plants.

Trench composting can be adapted to the size of your yard and how often you want to add food scraps. The only difference between pit and trench composting is the shape. You can think of pit composting as a circular hole in the ground. Trench composting looks more like a rectangle. After you try a few methods, you may develop your own technique that works best for your lifestyle.

Pit Composting

Pit composting involves digging a hole at least 1 foot deep (up to 2 feet if you are in a digging mood) and filling it 4 to 6 inches with food scraps and leaves. Fill the remainder of the hole with the soil you removed. Pit composting is a bit less organized than trench composting; usually you just bring a few days' worth of scraps out to your garden, dig a hole, drop the scraps, and bury them. Think of it as the "dig and drop" method.

The hardest part of pit composting, if you can even call it "hard," is remembering where you dug your pits so you don't dig it up before the material decomposes. Since underground composting relies on anaerobic bacteria, the process can emit unpleasant odors, which you won't smell unless you dig into the

---

Suggested Simple Compost Pile Recipe

3 parts leaves

1 part green yard trimmings

---

material before it has completely decomposed. If this idea troubles you, mark the piles with old popsicle sticks or some other marker. You could even get really organized and date the sticks so you know when you buried the material.

Choose an area of the garden not currently in use. As the materials decompose, they temporarily draw nitrogen out of the surrounding soil, and that could affect a sensitive plant nearby. Pit composting works best in beds you intend to plant next year that need a little more humus material.

Simple Garden Row Trenches

If you have a garden with rows, organize your trench composting into two stages. During one season, dig your trenches and bury the scraps and leaves in between the rows, where you walk. This allows the scraps many months to a year to decompose before you plant again. The next year, plant in your now-amended trench rows and add scraps to the rows you planted in the previous year. Rotating the trenches amends the soil and gives you an easy method to keep track of your trench composting.

PIT COMPOSTING

Let's Do It ➜

1

Dig a pit at least 1 foot deep.

2

Fill the bottom of the pit with 4 to 6 inches of food scraps and leaves.

3

Fill the rest of the pit with soil. If you want, mark the location with a popsicle stick. Wait six months to a year before planting over the top.

Keeping Critters Out of Your Deep Trench

MOST UNDERGROUND methods discussed in this section involve immediately topping your buried treasure with at least 5 inches of topsoil. This should discourage most nosy animal neighbors from digging into your compost. However, the deep trench method has only 1 inch of soil over food scraps for an extended period of time, sometimes a few weeks. If you know that raccoons, squirrels, or even dogs frequent your yard, you may need additional fortification to protect your compost.

After adding the 1 inch of soil, you could temporarily cover the area with chicken wire or another type of fencing you may have on hand. You could even use thick cardboard for the job. Weigh down the two sides with rocks or something else too heavy for our furry friends to lift. Look around and get creative. I spoke with one gardener who covered his garden trench with an old heavy door until he was finished adding food scraps.

Aside from a physical barrier, you could place an olfactory barrier. Covering the soil with a layer of coffee grounds will not only add to the compost but also deter some animals. Ammonia also acts as an olfactory deterrent. Most wild animals (and most humans for that matter) dislike the stringent smell of ammonia. You can place a small open container of ammonia on the pile or tie strips of rags soaked in ammonia nearby. Ammonia does burn plants, though, so be careful to not allow the ammonia to touch plant leaves.

Deeper Trench

Another method involves digging a deeper trench of 18 to 24 inches. Sprinkle food scraps and leaves in and cover with 1 inch of soil. Continue to add food scraps and leaves, and with each addition, cover the trench with another 1 inch of soil. This slow layering will usually last a period of a few weeks, depending on how quickly you generate food scraps. When you have filled in food scraps and soil within 5 inches of the top, stop adding food scraps. Fill in the remaining 5 inches with soil and mound more soil over the top. As the food scraps lose water and decompose, the area will settle. Next year, you will have well-amended soil for planting.

Let's Do It ➜

1
Dig a deep trench that measures at least 18 inches. Most deep trenches have lengths of 4 to 6 feet, about long enough to lay down in. Avoid digging this trench after dark or you may raise suspicion among nosy neighbors concerned you are not just composting but covertly disposing of a body.

2
Add food scraps to the trench and layer with leaves and other compostables, such as plant trimmings.

3
Cover with 1 inch of soil. Temporarily cover the trench with a protective barrier, such as fencing, if needed (see sidebar).

4
Continue this layering over a few weeks until you have filled within 5 inches of the top.

5
Fill the top 5 inches with soil and mound more soil over the top to allow for setting.

6
Wait six months to a year before planting on top of the trench.

The Deeper Trench method allows you to do more digging at one time and then use the same trench for a few weeks. Depending on the soil conditions and bedrock where you live, digging 24 inches into the ground with only a shovel may prove difficult. Only attempt to dig a trench with unfrozen soil. Too many rocks or too much impenetrable clay may require an aerobic workout and a sharp shovel to break through, but the end result of more fertile soil for your plants is worth a little sweat.

The English Method

We can thank the English for delicious tea, the Beatles, and of course, a very structured method of trench composting sometimes referred to as "The English Method" or "The Rotating Method." This solution works well in a limited space. The English Method divides the garden into three sections: the composting trench, the walking path, and the planting area. Each area rotates through over a 3-year period, so your composting trench becomes a walking path and then a planting area.

Let's Do It ➜

1
Map out your garden space to divide rows into three categories: composting trench, walking path, and planting area.

2
During the first year, fill the composting trench with food scraps as you would in the Simple Garden Row trench method. Dig at least 1 foot deep and cover with at least 5 inches of soil. Use the other two rows as a walking path and a planting path.

3
During the second year, convert the composting trench to a walking space and the planting trench to a composting trench. Follow the same method as before regarding depth and soil cover.

4
During the third year, rotate the trenches again so the composting trench from your first year is now your planting trench.

This method gives your food scraps plenty of time to decompose and also means you will not be walking on the squishy ground of buried compost as you would with the Simple Garden Row method. If this rotating technique seems too complicated for you, defer to the Deeper Trench or Simple Garden Row method. However, if you seek to eventually supplement all your garden's soil and improve drainage in an organized fashion, perhaps you should give it a try.

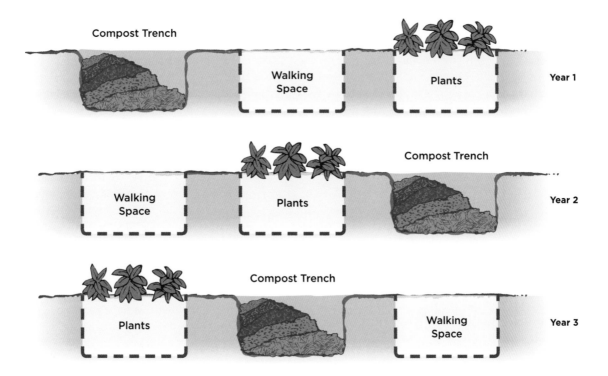

The English or rotating method of trench composting takes an organized approach to moving the trenches around the garden.

What to Expect with Trench Composting

Since this type of composting technically falls under the cold composting category and is often anaerobic, your materials will take longer to decompose than with a hotter method. Depending on the type of food scraps you place in your pit or trench, the organisms in the soil, the season, and your climate, what you bury will become unrecognizable in six months. This is cold composting; it takes longer because the microbial activity is lower and the compost generally doesn't heat up.

Pit and trench composting work well in sandy soil because the water in food scraps can easily drain away. These methods also do well in hot, dry climates where composters face difficulties keeping their aboveground compost piles moist enough. However, composters with all types of soil can enjoy the benefits of underground composting; some may need a sharper shovel and a stronger back.

Even though this composting takes place underground, you still need to watch the carbon and nitrogen mix of materials. Only adding food scraps will result in slower decomposition than also adding dry leaves or other brown materials.

In most cases, wait a year to plant material on top of your pit or trench. High-carbon material will call upon the nitrogen reserves in the soil to decompose. Conversely, the high-nitrogen materials may release the wrong form of nitrogen right away. Waiting to plant for a year will make sure the material properly decomposes, making the nitrogen available for plants. If you must plant on top of the trench, add bone or blood meal to the pile before you cover with soil to give a nitrogen boost.

One downside of underground composting is that the material may not get hot enough to kill seeds in the food scraps or plants you add. You may notice peppers and tomato plants coming up from your rotten vegetables. If volunteer plants bother you, try digging the trench even deeper. Most seeds buried at least 1 foot deep will eventually decompose with no hope of sprouting to the surface.

Suggested Trench Composting Recipe

3 parts shredded leaves

1 part food scraps

1 cup cottonseed meal, alfalfa meal, or blood meal per 20 pounds of material

Grasscycling

Freshly mowed grass clippings provide a fantastic source of water and nitrogen for your backyard compost. That said, I rarely ever add grass clippings to my compost pile. Why? I am practical and maybe a little lazy. I grasscycle. If you are also practical, lazy, and enjoy having green grass, you too will want to consider grasscycling.

Grasscycling technically falls outside of the traditional composting definition but only because it is so easy to do. Instead of raking up grass clippings, adding them to the compost, and then applying finished compost to your lawn, you just leave the clippings to decompose where they fall. Grasscycling allows all the nitrogen and other nutrients in the clippings to seep into the ground under the grass, essentially feeding the grass with itself. Grass clippings provide as much as one-third of your lawn's fertilizer needs.

Although easy, you do need to follow a few basic rules when grasscycling.

1 Know your ideal mowing height. Your local extension office or gardening club can tell you the best mowing height for grass in your area. For example, where I live, the proper mowing height is 3 inches. This height allows grass in my climate to maintain a healthy amount of water and perform a necessary level of photosynthesis.

2 Mow regularly. If you allow the grass to grow too tall and then have to slice too much of the blade off when you mow, that weakens the grass and leaves large clumps of grass behind that may smother the still-living grass below. Mow often enough that you only remove one-third of the leaf surface at any time. In my example, I should not let my grass grow higher than 4 inches before I shave a little off the top.

3 Mow dry grass only. As you probably know, mowing wet grass creates messy clumps that will decompose more slowly than fine sprinkles. If you have to mow in wet conditions, you can break up the clumps with a rake to speed up decomposition. Easy peasy. Just mow your grass and leave the clippings behind to decompose into the lawn. If life gets away from you and you find yourself mowing more of a jungle than a lawn, rake up the trimmings and add them to your compost. Specially designed mulching mowers make grasscycling even easier by shredding the blades of grass very small before spitting them out onto your lawn. Reel mowers also work well for grasscycling since they can only effectively cut a small amount of the blade at a time, and they drop the cuttings in place instead of spitting them out to the side.

Grass clippings left on your lawn will supply nutrients to the grass plants.

Grasscycling Does Not Create Thatch

SOME PEOPLE rake their grass clippings for fear of creating thatch, a nasty layer of tightly interwoven living and dead stems and roots that develops between the grass and the soil. Grass clippings do not contribute to thatch because water makes up 75 to 85 percent of their structure and they decompose so quickly. Other parts of the grass plant, such as the stems and the roots, can create thatch because they decompose so slowly.

RECOMMENDED MOWING HEIGHTS FOR COMMON GRASS TYPES

Centipede grass	1.0 to 2.0 inches
Common bermudagrass	1.0 to 2.0 inches
Hybrid bermudagrass	1.0 to 1.5 inches
Tall fescue	2.0 to 3.0 inches
St. Augustine grass	2.0 to 3.0 inches
Zoysia grass	1.0 to 2.0 inches

Source: University of Georgia Cooperative Extension

African Keyhole Gardens

Finished compost provides your garden with numerous benefits, but what if you could also reap benefits from your compost while the pile decomposes too? African keyhole gardens place composting in the center of a small-scale raised bed. The plants in the bed benefit from the nutrient-rich runoff coming from the pile and the increase in macro- and microorganisms drawn by the compost. The compost benefits from the insulation of the bin and the shared organisms. Everyone is happy and everyone wins, including you.

Construction of African keyhole gardens is limited only by your imagination. Most gardeners building them use found or leftover materials, including bricks, rocks, and pavers. The key is to create a raised bed with a compost bin in the center. Ideally the compost bin is made from wire or mesh, allowing easy transfer of moisture and organisms with the surrounding soil. Instead of creating a perfectly circular garden bed, notch the circle with a keyhole to give access to the compost bin in the center. That way you can easily walk up to the compost and deposit materials without needing to reach over a garden bed.

As their name implies, African keyhole gardens originated in Africa as a way to intensively grow vegetables in a manner that retains moisture and reduces the need for watering. Anyone in a hot or dry climate will benefit from building one of these gardens, but raised garden beds offer benefits we can all appreciate.

This African keyhole garden uses wood and grapevines to form a natural-looking center compost bin.

DIY AFRICAN KEYHOLE GARDEN

Materials Needed:

1 Sharp shovel
2 String or measuring tool
3 Compost bin for center (mesh works well)
4 Soil
5 Material for outside wall (brick, stone, etc.)
6 Creativity

Suggested African Keyhole Garden Composting Recipe

6 parts straw or shredded leaves

1 part manure and bedding

1 part food scraps

1 part green plant trimmings

Let's Do It →

1
First, clear an area for the bed and measure two circles. The first inner circle will be the composting area and should measure between 1 and 3 feet in diameter. The outer circle should measure 6 feet in diameter.

2
Notch the outer circle with a keyhole patch large enough for you to access the compost in the center.

3
Create the compost basket or bin first. A simple wire mesh bin such as the Wire Leaf Bin in Chapter 5 works perfectly. I've seen people in Uganda expertly weaving the inner compost basket from strong bamboo-like poles and bendable branches. Use materials to which you have easy access. Remember that soil will surround this bin, so it needs to be strong enough to withstand the weight. If you use wire mesh, reinforce the mesh with vertical pieces of wood to support the weight or loop the mesh into multiple layers to increase the strength.

4
Once a sturdy bin is ready, build the outside wall. You can use bricks, stones, pavers, or pretty much any material you can stack in a circle to create a bed. I have even seen beds made out of wine and beer bottles set in mortar, a resourceful way to use a potentially plentiful material (depending on your drinking habits).

5
Fill the compost bin with material first to further increase the strength of the bin. You can add all the same materials you would add to a regular backyard composting setup.

6
Fill in the surrounding bed with soil and compost. Traditionally, builders of African keyhole gardens line the bottom and sides of the bed with a thick layer of cardboard or other water-resistant material before adding soil. The layer acts to hold in water in hot, dry climates but is unnecessary in temperate regions.

7
Plant what your heart desires. Many African keyhole gardens contain vegetables, but you could plant flowers, herbs, or any smaller landscaping plant you choose. When the bed needs watering, water the center compost bin and allow the water to trickle down to the rest of the bed.

8
Some African keyhole gardens have modest walls, while others stretch 3 feet high or taller. The height depends on your landscape and resources. A taller outside wall will allow you to fill the bed with more soil and reap more benefit from the interior compost bin. I've seen shorter outside walls holding in a small mound of soil with the peak of the hill cresting at the compost pile.

9
Depending on the depth of your African keyhole garden bed, you will occasionally need to dig out the finished compost from the inner bin. For most setups, digging out the material once per year will prove sufficient. You only need to ensure you have enough space to continue adding compostables.

African Keyhole Garden
Overhead View

African Keyhole Garden
Side View Cutout

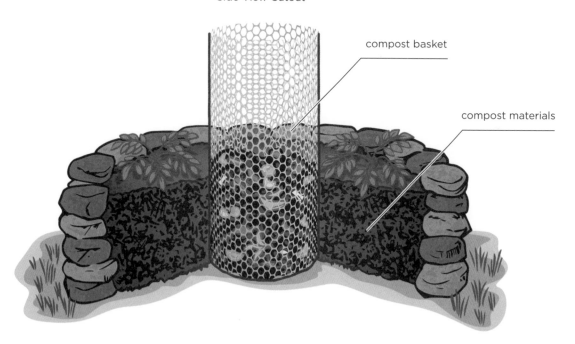

compost basket

compost materials

The compost pile in the center of an African keyhole garden provides continuous nutrients and water to the surrounding plants.

Hugelkultur

Most backyard composting methods shy away from large branches and logs since they take so long to decompose. Not so with Hugelkultur composters, who use rotting logs as the basis for a raised bed supported by a mound of compost. Hugelkultur (pronounced *hoo-gul-culture*) uses the very gradual decay of wood to act as a long-term supply of nutrients to the plants above. People in Germany and Eastern Europe (hence the German word for "hill culture" or "mound culture") have practiced this technique for centuries, but permaculture experts recently perfected the technique and have started encouraging others to take up the practice.

Gardeners using this method say that beyond nutrients, the decaying wood (and other materials) generates heat, extending the growing season for the plants. The branches and logs breaking down aerate the soil so the gardener never has to till the area. Decaying wood also acts as a sponge, soaking up water during rainy times and slowly releasing water during drier times. Most plants would appreciate this slow-release watering.

Constructing a Hugelkultur bed does take some time and hard work, but reaping the benefits of the decaying material for the next 20 years seems worth the effort.

compost/soil

leaves/grasses

rotten wood

brush/twigs

softwoods

hardwoods

Hugelkultur uses large wood and other slow-decomposing materials to create a long-lasting garden bed with self-watering benefits.

DIY HUGELKULTUR BED

Materials Needed:

1 Sharp shovel
2 Hardwood and/or softwood logs and branches
3 Soil

Let's Do It →

1
First, dig a 1-foot-deep trench a few feet wide. The bed can measure any length and width you choose.

2
Fill the trench with hardwood on the bottom and then with softwood if you have both. The hardwoods will decay more slowly and the softwoods more quickly, so a mix is nice, but any wood combination will work. Avoid black walnut and black locust since they release potentially toxic chemicals (for your plants) as they decompose.

3
Continue filling the trench with any bulky organic material you would like to compost. Remember, you can break the rules with Hugelkultur. Tough roots, shrubs, and vines are all fair game. Over the tougher materials, add more traditional compostables such as leaves, straw, and manure. You can mound as high as you would like.

Some people create crazy vertical gardens using this technique reaching 6 feet tall or higher.

4
Cover your materials with 6 inches of topsoil.

5
During the first year of your Hugelkultur bed, the decomposing materials will steal much of the nitrogen from the surrounding soil. If you want to plant on the bed immediately, you will need to supplement the soil with a high-nitrogen material such as blood meal, manure, or high-nitrogen fertilizer. Or you can simply allow the mound to rest for a year before planting. Although the tough layers will continue to decompose, a mature mound should provide as much or more nitrogen than it robs from your plants.

Hugelkultur beds work well in areas with very poor soil where you are pretty much "starting from scratch" as far as building up a garden. Gardeners who prefer not to water a bed regularly will also find a benefit in the slow-release, sponge-like rotting wood under the bed. Since these beds look like a mound, they also add some interesting height to your garden, which could spice up your landscaping.

When using varieties listed in the "Okay" column, you should only add them when they're well-rotted or aged so they do not sprout and are less likely to release antimicrobial chemicals. Most species in this column have a strong resistance to decay, meaning they will last in your mound for a long time. Those species in the "Avoid" column include black locust, which will not decompose in your lifetime; black walnut, which contains the plant-toxic chemical juglone; and old-growth redwoods, which have persistent chemicals that can prevent seed germination.

This Hugelkultur bed created last year is now ready for plants.

WOOD SELECTION FOR HUGELKULTUR

Best	Okay	Avoid
Alder	Black cherry	Black locust
Apple	Camphor	Black walnut
Aspen	Cedar	Old-growth redwood
Birch	Eucalyptus	
Cottonwood	Fir	
Maple	Juniper	
Oak	Osage orange	
Poplar	Pacific yew	
	Pine or spruce	
	Red mulberry	
	Willow	

Suggested Recipe for Hugelkultur

Mix of hardwood and softwood logs and branches, enough to fill a trench 1 to 2 feet deep

1 part vines, twigs, and other tough materials

1 part manure

1 part leaves or straw

Topsoil dug from the trench

What Is Permaculture?

YOU MAY HAVE HEARD the term *permaculture* thrown around but may be unfamiliar what it really means. Permaculture is a way of thinking and designing that mimics patterns and relationships found in nature. The founders, David Holmgren and Bill Mollison, started permaculture in the mid-1970s, primarily focusing on landscape design to look at how and what we plant, but the concept has blossomed into many other areas. Deep thinkers can use the permaculture principles and ethics to examine all aspects of our lives, from energy to transportation to medicine.

Those following permaculture seek to creatively redesign our behavior and how we interact with the environment to use less energy and fewer resources while still providing for ourselves.

Permaculturists wish for us to become more self-reliant while creating a smaller environmental footprint. They look for practical and empowering solutions for everyday issues.

Backyard composting fits well with the permaculture philosophy because we are becoming more self-reliant while creating value from our byproducts (food scraps and yard trimmings). One of the 12 guiding principles of permaculture is "Produce No Waste." Backyard composting helps us step a little closer in that direction.

The 12 guiding principles are as follows:

1 Observe and interact
2 Catch and store energy
3 Obtain a yield
4 Apply self-regulation and accept feedback
5 Use and value renewable resources and services
6 Produce no waste
7 Design from patterns to details
8 Integrate rather than segregate
9 Use small and slow solutions
10 Use and value diversity
11 Use edges and value the marginal
12 Creatively use and respond to change

If permaculture intrigues you, I recommend reading further on the subject in *Permaculture: Principles and Pathways Beyond Sustainability* by David Holmgren, who co-originated the permaculture concept.

Shifting Compost Pile

If you have ever moved a compost bin or pile and looked at the soil underneath, you will understand the immense benefit a compost pile has to the surrounding soil. In the same way, a shifting compost pile moves (with your help) around your garden, leaving amended soil in its wake.

This method works especially well with hot composting, since the material needs frequent turning and will decompose quickly. Simply build the pile in an unplanted area of your garden (or on top of plants you want to smother). After a week or two, pull out the pitchfork and move the pile to a neighboring spot. After another week, migrate the pile another step further into the next neighboring spot. When you relocate the pile, you aerate the materials and speed up decomposition. Eventually, when the pile has decomposed to a ready-to-harvest compost, you can simply spread the material into the surrounding garden, eliminating the need for a wheelbarrow.

Let's Do It ➜

1

Start heaping up material in an area of your garden without plants or with plants you don't mind smothering. Add a good balance of green and brown material, knowing that any food scraps you add may attract pests.

2

Once enough material is in place, allow the pile a few weeks to heat up.

3

Using a pitchfork, move the pile from its current location to the space next to the pile. Think of a slinky going down the stairs. You are just moving it one step over.

4

Continue migrating the pile every week or two until it has finished decomposition.

5

Spread the finished compost into the surrounding garden.

Suggested Recipe for Shifting Compost Pile

3 parts shredded leaves

1 part yard trimmings, cut small

1 part manure with bedding

Using Shredded Leaves or Cardboard for Paths

ALTHOUGH not technically composting, you can allow shredded leaves to decompose in other areas of your garden and use them for practical purposes. If you find yourself with more shredded leaves than your compost bin (or bins) can contain, use the leaves as mulch on your garden paths. You will find that the act of walking on the leaves combined with the weather breaks them down quickly while preventing weeds from sprouting on the paths. Avoid spreading a layer of shredded leaves thicker than 3 inches so that roots from surrounding plants do not grow up into the layer. Roots growing up out of the soil will be more susceptible to damage from frost in the winter and heat in the summer.

Cardboard works well in some types of gardens but not all. In large veggie gardens or when Pinterest-worthy beauty is not your end goal, you can use cardboard in the garden both on paths and in areas where you want to suppress plant growth. Worms seem to particularly enjoy the taste of cardboard (no one has yet to ask them why, but some hypothesize that the "sweet" glue may attract the worms). This practical and decomposable garden tool will soak up water in utilitarian paths to leave your gardening boots a little less muddy. Cardboard works especially well in the Simple Garden Row trench composting method to make the path a little less squishy.

Sheet or Blanket Composting

If you have a patch of grass you want to turn into a garden bed or you have an area that you want to completely replant, sheet composting offers an easy solution. Sheet or blanket composting (also referred to as sheet mulching) layers leaves and other compostables on top of the soil (like a blanket), suppressing the existing plant growth and, after decomposition, offering a new, freshly amended bed.

Since one of the goals of sheet composting is to suppress or completely kill the plants underneath, sheet composting starts with a layer of newspaper or cardboard. This technique also tops the sheet with finished compost, which brings beneficial microorganisms to the area while also making the end result appear more like a garden bed and less like a giant compost pile.

Suggested Recipe for Sheet Compost

1 part black-and-white newspaper or cardboard without tape or staples

3 parts shredded brown leaves

2 parts straw

1 part manure

1 part food scraps

1 part yard trimmings

1 to 2 parts finished compost

1 part mulch

Let's Do It ➜

1
Chose an area of your lawn or an old bed you want to cover. Most sheet composting sites measure between 50 and 200 square feet, but you could go as small or large as you choose.

Blanket the area with a layer of newspaper or cardboard. Only use the black-and-white sections of the newspaper (no glossy inserts), and only use cardboard without tape or staples, since these will not decompose. You want at least one layer of cardboard or five layers of newspaper. The more layers you add, the better the chance that you will kill whatever plants live under the sheet.

2
Create the bulky layer using straw, leaves, yard trimmings, manure, and food scraps. Ultimately, 8 to 12 inches of material will form the best sheet. Straw, leaves, and other bulky material will comprise most of this layer. If you keep the brown-to-green balance in mind, you can layer whatever material you have.

3
Water the bulky layer.

4
Cover the sheet in 1 to 2 inches of compost if you have compost available. If not, the sheet will still work, just a little more slowly. You could also layer manure here for a nice punch of high-nitrogen material.

5
Add a final layer of mulch, shredded leaves, or other material that you do not mind looking at for the next six months to a year.

6
Keep the area moist with a soaker hose or regular watering. Straw and other bulky materials will easily dry out, slowing decomposition.

Sheet composting essentially takes a compost pile and spreads it out thickly over a large area. This technique requires a lot of material depending on the size of ground you cover. You will need an entire pickup truck full of material to cover an area measuring 50 square feet. This usually requires outsourcing your supply of materials. Savvy outsourcers come up with some creative ideas:

Bagged shredded leaves from neighbors

Spent coffee grounds from local coffee shops

Horse manure from horse farms, race tracks, equestrian schools, etc.

Spent straw from grocery stores or other shops using it as fall decoration

Pine needles from pop-up Christmas tree shops

You probably already thought of others available to you. Don't be shy about asking around. Most shop owners will greet your offer to take the moldy straw off their hands with a huge smile. Of course, a pickup truck does help with the task of carting manure and smelly, bulky material around town.

If you desire your new bed to have a certain shape, say a perfect rectangle, consider enclosing the outside of the sheet composting area. Short fencing or cedar planks will give the new bed crisper edges and keep the material contained. You can always remove these after the material has decomposed if you choose.

Once you have created your layers of sheet compost, you only need to check them occasionally to keep them from drying out. Keep the layers moist with a soaker hose or regular watering so the microorganisms thrive and happily do their work. Once the material decomposes, you have a lovely new bed to plant. No need to harvest or cart the material anywhere in a wheelbarrow.

What Plants Grow Well in Partially Decomposed Compost?

WHEN INTEGRATING compost into your garden, you may come to a point when you want to plant something before the material finishes decomposition. The right plants can thrive when integrated with sheet composting, Hugelkultur, or trench composting—you just need to know what plants can tolerate these conditions. While materials decompose, they consume all the available nitrogen, so any plant you wish to grow will either need to fix its own nitrogen, or you will need to supply extra nitrogen in the form of fertilizer.

Any plant from the legume family, such as beans, snap peas, and edamame, fixes nitrogen from the air, sometimes sourcing as much as 80 percent of their nitrogen this way. However, young plants will need a small amount of fertilizer until they grow large-enough leaves to fix most of the nitrogen they need. Alfalfa meal, blood meal, or bat guano products provide high amounts of nitrogen.

Squash, cucumber, and melon tend to thrive atop compost piles and will sometimes voluntarily sprout out of a traditional compost bin from the rotting scraps. Consider adding a trellis to grow cucumbers and squash vertically.

7

VERMICOMPOSTING

EASY AND FUN
INDOOR COMPOSTING

Imagine if you could keep hundreds, even thousands, of pets in your home that would happily live in a container small enough to fit under your sink. Now imagine that these pets were useful for more than just cuddling. They eat your table scraps without a fuss, and their poop, rather than being a gross byproduct, is actually one of the best soil amendments in the world.

These small, red wigglers can eat half their weight in food scraps every day.

Vermicomposting (also called worm bin composting or vermiculture) is a special kind of composting you can do inside your home rather than in your backyard. The specific worms used in vermicomposting, red wigglers, can eat up to half their body weight in kitchen scraps a day. When you get past the ick factor of keeping worms, the process is quite clean. No odors and no turning the compost, and the vermicasts created by the worms look a lot like coffee grounds.

Some people choose to vermicompost because they don't like going out to their backyard bin in the winter or they live in an apartment with no backyard. Others like the convenience of composting food scraps indoors and use their backyard bin for yard trimmings and leaves. Still others enjoy maintaining a worm bin with their children as a way to learn about biology and decomposition in nature.

Vermi Wormy

You cannot dig a few earthworms out of the ground, throw them into a box, and call it a worm bin. Vermicomposting systems demand a special kind of worm: *Eisenia fetida*, or red wigglers. These little red worms like living in shallow containers, consume a large amount of food scraps in a short time, tolerate a wide range of temperatures, and reproduce quickly when provided a nice habitat and continuous supply of food. Once adjusted to your worm bin, red wigglers can process half of their body weight in fruit and vegetable scraps every day. Since the average-sized bin holds a pound of worms, you could feed your worms a half pound of food scraps every day. Not-so-coincidentally, this capacity generally takes care of the scraps from a family of four.

The worms eat the food scraps and produce vermicastings (a.k.a. worm poop). This high-nitrogen manure mixes with other decaying matter in the worm bin to create vermicompost. Gardeners prize vermicompost for its nutrient-rich humus texture, and those without worm bins pay a pretty penny to use it as a soil amendment and fertilizer.

Creating a Mini Ecosystem

Although red wigglers are the stars of the show, they have a strong support network of other decomposers that help break down the food scraps. Your worm bin is a mini-ecosystem containing a whole food web of organisms. Food scraps and other organic matter fuel the system.

Single-cell bacteria and fungi offer the chief assistance for our worms. In fact, you can consider earthworms to be microbe farmers, creating an environment perfect for these helpful creatures. The digestive track of the worms spans almost the entire length of their bodies to give bacteria the time to break down the decaying matter. Because of the microbes, what leaves the worm is actually more nutrient-rich than what entered (at least from the perspective of a plant).

Other organisms such as mold, actinomycetes (a fungus-like bacteria), beetle mites, sowbugs, and even small flies will make an occasional appearance in your bin and consume the food scraps directly. Secondary consumers, such as springtails, protozoa, and feather-winged beetles eat your first-level consumers and add to the decomposition process. You may occasionally see predators in your bin such as centipedes, ants, and pseudoscorpians (don't worry, these "scorpions" are so tiny you can barely see them). I suggest removing any centipedes and ants you see since they may eat the "good guys."

Building Your Own Worm Bin

The containers people use for indoor worm composting vary almost as much as backyard bins. The space needs to be large enough to accommodate the colony of worms, their bedding, and food scraps and have some breathing room for good air flow. For a family of four, you generally need a box 1 foot to 18 inches deep, 2 feet wide, and 3 feet long.

The selection of premade worm bins on the market today come with clever brand names such as Worm Wigwam, Vermi-Hut, and Worm Factory. Some of these bins offer nice features that were designed to improve ease of harvesting the compost and adding the food scraps. If you want to splurge on a high-rise condo for your worms, I suggest reading the reviews of the particular model you desire. The function of premade bin features come with varying levels of success.

You can also build your own worm bin using plywood or a plastic storage container. Basically, a worm bin is a box with holes, a lid, and a way for liquids to drain. You can find plans for wood bins, but the container will remain moist most of the time, so a plastic bin will last longer. A shallow container between 12 and 18 inches deep works best because the bedding tends to compact in a deep container.

DIY WORM BIN

Making your own worm bin is super simple and a great project to do with kids. Because these plans use a plastic container, drill lots of air holes and drain holes to make sure your little worm friends have plenty of ventilation and excess moisture can escape. You can order red wigglers online or sometimes find them in a bait shop. Just make sure you are getting the right species (*Eisenia fetida*) or you could end up with worms that try to escape or simply die because they cannot survive in this type of bin.

Bedding choices include shredded newspaper, shredded cardboard, animal manure, leaf mold compost, or peat moss. You could run newspaper (black and white only) through a paper shredder or, even better, task your little kid helpers with ripping the papers by hand. Adding a few handfuls of shredded leaves will improve the appearance of the finished vermicompost, but it may also introduce predators, such as centipedes.

Red wigglers are naturally litter dwellers, so they don't tunnel through the soil like earthworms in our backyards. They prefer the shredded-paper-and-food-scrap habitat we create in the bin. You do need to add a handful of good living garden soil when preparing the bin to add grit. The worms use this grit in their gizzards to help break down the food scraps since they do not have teeth. This soil also inoculates the bin with bacteria, mold, and fungi to help in the composting process.

With amazingly simple anatomy, small but mighty worms are able to help decompose incredible volumes of material.

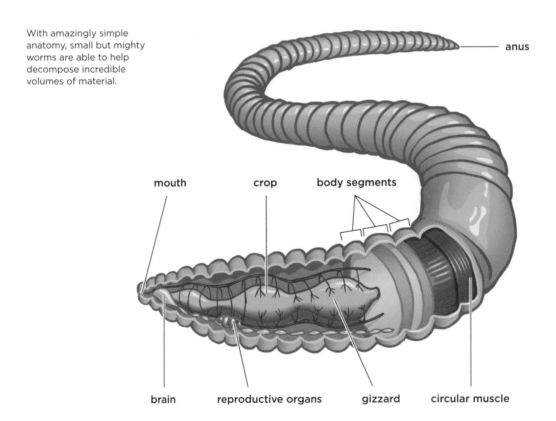

anus

mouth   crop   body segments

brain   reproductive organs   gizzard   circular muscle

Materials Needed:

1 1 plastic storage container (about 10 gallons; do not use clear)

2 2 plastic storage container lids

3 Drill

4 Shredded newspaper (about 5 pounds)

5 *Water*

6 *1 cup soil*

7 1 pound red wigglers (*Eisenia fetida*)

8 Gloves

9 Safety glasses

 Pictured    *Not shown*

Let's Do It →

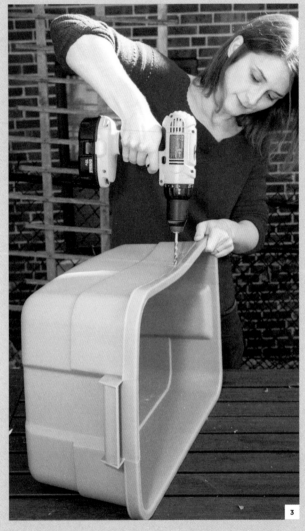

1

Fill a large bowl or small bucket with water and set it aside for a few hours to allow the chlorine to evaporate (or pull water from your rain barrel).

2

Turn the bin over and drill eighteen to twenty ¼" holes in the bottom of the worm bin for drainage. Space the drainage holes about 2 inches apart.

3

Create ventilation holes in the plastic bin by drilling ¼" holes along the top side of the bin. Keep the holes about 2" apart. Don't worry about the worms escaping; if you use the correct species and maintain the bin, these worms will happily stay inside.

4

Choose one of the lids to act as the lid of the bin (the other will act as the tray under the bin). Drill more ventilation holes around the lid of the bin, about 2" apart. About 15 to 20 holes will work. Remember, the worms need air, but they also prefer a dark environment. Too many holes will bring in too much light and hurt their little worm eyes (really, light receptors; worms do not have eyes).

5

Now gather your bedding material. I prefer shredded newspaper with a few handfuls of brown leaves. Soak the newspaper in the bowl or bucket of water you set aside in Step 1 until the pieces are saturated. Lift out the paper and wring it out so it is not dripping. You will need enough bedding to fill the bin three-quarters full. It will take more newspaper than you think: about ½ pound for every gallon capacity of your bin.

6

Transfer your soaked and wrung-out newspaper to the worm bin. Mix in soil and leaves, if desired, until the materials are evenly distributed.

7

Introduce the worms by gently spreading them out in the bin. Welcome home, wormies!

8

Now add some food scraps to the bin. The smaller the pieces are, the faster they will break down. Start with ¼ pound of food scraps.

9

Cover all the food scraps with bedding to avoid fruit flies.

10

Set the undrilled lid onto your work surface to act as a leachate tray. Place a spacer material, such as a few bricks or blocks of wood, in between the bin and leachate tray. These spacers hold the bin up off the leachate tray, allowing for drainage and air flow. Rest the bin on the spacers.

Your worms will be in shock at first. Think about your first time living in a new home or your first day at a new job. The worms may need some time to adjust before you can ramp up their food, so start slowly and take a break if you see too many food scraps building up.

Taking Care of Your New Pets

Although you are unlikely to name the 1,000+ new housemates you are keeping, they are live animals that require some basic needs met to thrive. You will need to consider the following:

- Temperature
- Ventilation
- Moisture
- Acidity

Temperature: Keep your worm bin at a temperature between 55 and 77°F. Because the bedding is wet, it can freeze more easily than the surrounding air. Temperatures below 50°F will significantly slow down the worm activity. Temperatures above 84°F will likely prove fatal to the worms. The best places to store your worms to avoid the temperature extremes tend to be non-drafty basements or garages or, if you can convince the rest of your family, right under the kitchen sink.

Ventilation: Worms "breathe" through their skin and create carbon dioxide and other gases like any living organism. They must have fresh air, or they will eventually smother and die. Provide plenty of air holes in the bin and never wrap the bin in a plastic bag. When you add the food scraps, fluff up the bedding to circulate the air in the bin.

Moisture: We added water to the bedding because worms need to keep their skin wet in order to "breathe" or exchange air. Too much water will drown the worms, though, so keep an eye on the moisture and maintain a wrung-out sponge level of dampness in the bin.

Acidity: Worms can survive a fairly wide range of pH, between 5 and 9. (Neutral pH is 7.) Be careful not to add anything too acidic, such as lots of lemon peels, or you could bring the acidity to dangerous levels. Often, if you see worms trying to escape the bin, the habitat is either too acidic or too wet.

This may make worms seem like high-maintenance pets, but once you have these basics down, the worms are fairly easy to keep alive. You can leave a worm bin untouched for a few weeks and go back to worms still munching away. If you intend to vacation for a month or more, I would recommend boarding your worms with a sympathetic friend.

Sprouting Avocado Pits

OF ALL THE "healthy" foods out there, avocado may be my favorite. Most of us can't resist a freshly sliced avocado on a salad or a nice lime- and cilantro-laden bowl of guacamole. You may have held the lovely round avocado pit before and contemplated growing your own avocado plant from the seed, perhaps starting a small avocado forest that would provide you a continuous supply of creamy, good-for-you fats. And, if you're like most people, you probably failed in your avocado-sprouting attempt.

Your vermicomposting bin has a secret. Because of the plant-growth stimulating qualities of vermicompost and the moist environment, avocado pits tend to easily germinate after a few months in your worm bin.

The process is easy:

1 Put the avocado pit in the worm bin.
2 Wait for it to sprout.
3 Pull it out and plant it in a big pot with sandy soil.

Unless you live in a hot climate or have a greenhouse-type room in your home, you may not actually harvest any avocados. Regardless, avocados make a pretty house plant and a perfect conversation starter.

Feeding Your Worms

Worms will eat any kitchen scraps you have, but start with fresh fruit and vegetable scraps as a novice vermicomposter. Chopping up dense scraps, such as broccoli stems, will make munching easier for your worms. Start by adding these basic scraps:

- Potato peels
- Banana peels
- Outside leaves from lettuce and cabbage
- Celery ends
- Onion peels
- Apple and pear cores
- Tea leaves
- Coffee grounds
- Tomato stems

You get the idea. Any parts leftover from cutting fruits and vegetables. Spent coffee grounds and tea leaves also make easy additions. You can start adding rotten vegetables found at the back of the produce drawer once you feel confident with the novice list. If you have 1 pound of worms, you can add up to ½ pound of food a day—think five banana peels or half a head of lettuce.

Add leftover cooked vegetables without oil and grains in moderation. Too much cooked food can start giving your bin a garbage odor. Slimy or moldy food is fine, but you may want to avoid large amounts of broccoli, cabbage, onion, and other strong-smelling vegetables since they tend to also smell more when decomposing.

Just as when you are backyard composting, you must bury food scraps after you add them. This will keep fruit flies from laying eggs on scraps at the surface or hatching if the larvae are already on your food. I keep a garden fork near the worm bin and simply lift a layer of bedding before dumping the scraps.

Although you can experiment with most food, there are a few types of scraps you should not add to your bin.

- Meat and bones: Meat creates foul odors as it decomposes and attracts unwanted guests to the bin.
- Citrus peels: A few are okay, but citrus peels can lower the pH of the bin and also seem to attract little white mites. I avoid these completely but know some vermicomposters who add citrus in moderation.
- Dog and cat feces: Manure from your non-worm pets will not only stink but will also add harmful pathogens to the final compost.

Mary Appelhof, author of *Worms Eat My Garbage,* developed a creative technique for adding food scraps to your worm bin that allows material to break down in an organized and systematic fashion. She divides the bin into nine theoretical segments and keeps a record sheet of where she places the food scraps each day. By rotating the food scraps around the bin, you can assess how quickly your worms have eaten the scraps in the first cell on the tenth day. If after 10 days the scraps in the first cell are completely intact, you will need to slow down adding food scraps until the worms have had a chance to reproduce. If you cannot see or can barely see the food scraps left, then you are right on track with how much you are adding.

Mary Appelhof devised a systematic approach to feeding worms so you can recognize when to slow down the feeding frequency.

The Kinky Sex Life of Worms

YOU MAY WONDER if you have to continuously buy more worms or if they will self-populate your worm bin. If you keep the habitat moist and at a neutral pH and feed the worms on a regular basis, they will reproduce faster than a basket of bunnies.

Red wigglers have both male and female parts. Once sexually mature, they develop a large clitellum, a band easily visible about one-third down the length of their bodies. If you imagine the worm as a horse, this would be the saddle. The ovaries and testes are located a short distance away from the clitellum, closer to the head. Even though they are hermaphroditic, they cannot self-fertilize. In this case, it really does take two to tango.

When they are in the mood, so to speak, they find any other worm and crawl alongside each other with their heads facing in opposite directions (a worm "69" that really looks more like an "11"). Both worms secrete mucus from their clitella and transfer sperm down their bodies and into the sperm storage sacks of the other worm. This mucus and sperm exchange lasts about three hours. Worms exhibit impressive stamina.

Later, a cocoon forms on each worm, and they wriggle out of the hardening cocoon while also depositing their eggs and their mate's sperm into the cocoon. Once off the worm, the cocoon closes on both ends, and inside, the sperm fertilize the eggs. Each cocoon carries several eggs, which form into hatchlings and grow for about three months inside the cocoon.

Red wigglers can create a cocoon every 14 to 21 days, but don't be alarmed. The worm population will self-regulate.

Harvesting Your Vermicompost

There are two schools of thought when it comes to harvesting vermicompost. Some people choose the "lazy route" which involves, as you might expect, less work, but you will lose most, if not all, of your worms. You can choose to feed your worms for period of time (at least six months) and then stop feeding them altogether. If you leave the worm bin unattended for a few months, the worms will eat all the food scraps, stop reproducing, and eventually starve to death and die, becoming part of your vermicompost. You will then have a container full of finished vermicompost you can use, but you will have to buy more worms to start a new bin.

If you prefer a less-macabre method of harvesting vermicompost, you will need to separate the worms from the compost. This is a more time-intensive process than harvesting backyard compost, but the payoff is worth the effort. I have harvested vermicompost using multiple techniques, and the following steps involve the least amount of work for the greatest reward. You will know your bin is ready to harvest when you see lots of dark brown vermicompost that looks like heaps of coffee grounds.

Let's Do It ➜

1
Take a plastic mesh bag that formerly held produce such as oranges and potatoes. Fill the bag with food scraps and bury the bag on one side of the bin.

2
Wait about 2 weeks and most of your wormies will have migrated to that side of the bin. Do not add food scraps anywhere else during those few weeks.

3
Pull the bag out (with a few hundred hanging worms) and place it in a temporary holding bucket. Cover the bucket to make the area dark and keep the worms happy.

4

Now you have a bin with most of the worms removed, but some will still be left. Spread out a tarp and create cone-shaped piles of your vermicompost on the tarp. This works best outside on a sunny day. The light-adverse worms will travel to the bottom of the piles. Be patient; the worms are slow.

5

While you wait for the worms to migrate, start your next bin with some fresh, moist bedding and leaves, following the steps on page 144. Add the worms lured by the food bag into their new home.

6

After a half hour or more, the remaining worms will have all migrated deeper into the cone-shaped piles. You can scrape off the tops of the cones using a shovel (or your hands) into a bucket. Shape the now-topless piles into new cones and wait again.

7

Eventually, I grow tired of the cone shaping and decide to just get in there and finish the process. I have a leave-no-man-behind attitude when it comes to harvesting vermicompost. This requires a few hours of quiet contemplation as I sift through the remainder of the compost. Wearing gloves, I pick up the worms (and sow bugs and millipedes) and gently toss them into the new bin. I go through each pile, spreading out the compost and picking up the little wiggly friends. What is left behind I happily scoop into my harvest bucket.

At any point in the cone-scrape-shape method, you could decide to just toss the remaining vermicompost and worms back into your "new" bin (gently!). A little of the finished vermicompost actually helps jumpstart your new bin with microbes.

If you want to harvest compost in the winter or on a rainy day, you could set up a table with a tarp in your basement for the harvest. You will need a very bright light (or a few) to mimic the sun and encourage the worms to migrate lower in your cone-shaped piles.

A nice bonus of this method is that you can stretch the harvesting out over several days and just go down and scrape off the tops of the cones every once in a while. Red wigglers are not native worms to most of the world. Just tossing the worms and their finished compost into your garden could result in introducing an alien species. The worms would likely not survive a cold winter if you have one, but it is still not worth the risk.

Using Your Worm Poop

Now that you have harvested your "black gold," you will want to reap the benefits. Vermicompost may as well be a plant superhero; it offers so many fantastic benefits. The spongy quality of vermicompost aerates and increases the water retention of the soil. In a wonder of nature, the vermicastings coming out of the worm actually have more beneficial bacteria than the food they eat or that are in the worm's gut. The humic acid present in the vermicompost makes nutrients and micronutrients such as calcium, iron, potassium, sulfur, and phosphorus more readily available for plant absorption. Vermicompost stimulates plant growth (a great reason to use it in starting seeds), and the microbes present help protect plants from disease. Give it some Spandex and a cape, and vermicompost could hold a place in the Avengers lineup.

You will not have as large a quantity of compost as you do after harvesting a backyard bin. That's okay. Vermicompost is super concentrated in nutrients, and a little goes a long way.

Many vermicomposters use their compost for starting seedlings or transplanted baby plants in a vegetable garden. Simply dust a layer of vermicompost in your seed row after you have laid down the seeds. Scoop a small amount of vermicompost into the hole you dig for a transplant. You don't need very much to make an impact.

Vermicompost also makes an excellent topdressing for houseplants and in the garden. Sprinkle some around the top of a plant and the nutrients will work their way into the soil. If you want to use vermicompost when potting a new plant, use at least two-thirds potting soil to one-third vermicompost. You really don't need more than that, so spread the love around your plants.

Adult black soldier flies live only long enough to mate and lay eggs.

Black Soldier Fly Larvae Composting

MOST NORMAL PEOPLE try to avoid flies in their homes and around their yard, but with a new type of composting, people actually encourage black soldier flies to live and reproduce in their compost bins. Don't think of the large buzzing house flies or the annoying fruit flies. Black soldier flies tend to not hang around your home or, more importantly, your food because they only mate and lay eggs as adults living just a few days. Your compost bin is the perfect place for them to lay their eggs because of the readily available food scraps that will feed their big hungry babies (a.k.a. maggots or grubs).

These adorable babies process a serious amount of your food scraps very quickly, using your food scraps to grow and making you happy in the process. Black soldier flies spend five to eight days as adults, existing only to mate and lay eggs. The eggs take about four days to hatch, and then the larvae or maggots live for about two weeks. This is when they will eat and eat and eat your food scraps. Next, the larvae bury themselves and pupate for about two weeks before emerging as adults. Black soldier flies do not spread disease, and the adults cannot bite or sting.

Keeping black soldier flies is a type of farming, much like beekeeping, and while you don't get to wear the full protective beekeeper suit, you can create a special setup for the flies. These homes consist of an area for the females to lay their eggs (the delivery room), space for the larvae to eat (the nursery), drainage to pull off the leachate, and a chute where adults or almost-adults can separate themselves from the larvae. Like most backyard composting units, you can purchase premade systems or build one yourself. They can be scaled for backyard use and even commercial use.

Some composters forgo the fancy setup and just use a regular backyard compost bin. You can encourage natural black soldier flies to populate the bin, or you can buy the larvae to add to your bin. Black soldier flies do not, however, tolerate very cold winters, so if Jack Frost annually visits your area, black soldier flies may not hang around all year.

Black soldier fly farming/composting is not yet mainstream, but it is a growing trend among people who keep backyard chickens. The larvae shells from the black soldier flies make great chicken feed (though to be fair, chickens are not known for their discerning palates). Some people also use them for fishing bait. If you can get over the heebie-jeebie feeling of seeing a bunch of white squirming maggots eating your food scraps, black soldier fly farming may be for you.

TROUBLESHOOTING VERMICOMPOSTING ISSUES

Problem	Cause	Solution
Fruit flies are bothersome.	• Food is not buried under bedding material.	• Bury food scraps well. • Make a fruit fly trap (see page 80). • Hang sticky fly traps nearby. • Set the bin outside if weather permits.
Bedding dries out too quickly.	• Bin has too much ventilation.	• Spray water in the bin. • Keep the lid secure. • Change the location to a less-ventilated area
Water collects in the bottom of the bin.	• Bin has poor ventilation.	• Leave the lid off for a while. • Add a little new bedding and fluff with garden fork. • Change the location for better ventilation. • Reduce the amount of food added.
Mites are overpopulated in the bin.	• A food item you placed in the bin harbored mites.	• Place a slice of white bread in the bin to attract them. The next day, pull out the white bread with all the mites.
Mold is growing in the bin.	• Mold spores were on material you added.	• This isn't a big problem; you can leave it alone if you chose. • Turn the mold under material and bury it.
Bin is emitting bad odors.	• Food is not buried under bedding material. • Too many food scraps have been added. • Dairy, meat, or oily food scraps were added.	• Do not feed scraps to worms for a week. • Add dry bedding. • Bury all food scraps. • Do not add dairy or meat food scraps.

8

HARVESTING
AND USING
YOUR FINISHED
COMPOST

ALL GOOD THINGS COME
TO THOSE WHO WAIT

After a few months (or a few weeks for you hot composters), you will inevitably want to harvest your brown gold. We could become philosophical and say that composting, like life, is more about the journey and not the destination and that your months of work tending to your compost pile, adding food scraps and leaves, checking moisture levels, and aerating when needed were the true joys of a backyard composter. But that would be absurd.

Beautiful, crumbly compost ready for your garden.

You would not make a delicious batch of chocolate chip cookies and then refuse to eat at least one. Although we enjoy all the steps of composting, harvesting your finished compost takes the cake as the best day in a composter's life. At least the composting part of your life (we are not that sad). Digging into the compost pile to reveal crumbly dark brown humus with a sweet, earthy scent may be more satisfying than eating a warm cookie right out of the oven. Maybe.

Are We There Yet?

Deciding when your compost has finished decomposition does not require a degree in soil science. If the material is not steaming and no longer resembles the original banana peel, you can call it finished. Some fragments of partially decomposed wood and other tough fibers hang on, but they add a nice texture to the compost that most plants will appreciate.

With several composting methods, such as a compost tumbler, the material leaving the bin may not have entered the final, longer stage of decomposition. No need to worry. This material will continue to decompose after you use it in your garden.

Expect to harvest compost from a traditional contained backyard unit once or twice per year.

Typically, I harvest my compost in the fall to make room for the influx of leaves. I will harvest small amounts again in the spring for new beds or to help seedlings. The average backyard compost pile or bin will create one heaping wheelbarrow full of compost a year. It provides enough to spread a ½-inch layer over about 300 square feet.

If you use the hot composting method, you could harvest compost every few months, but this method takes a level of time and dedication most composters, myself included, do not have. Tumblers also generate finished compost faster than other methods, so expect to create finished compost every few months with a tumbler as well.

Harvesting Compost from a Single-Bin Unit

Single-unit composters win the crown as the most common type of backyard composting. If you only have one backyard compost bin, you will need to follow a few special steps to harvest the material since you continually add food scraps on top of the finished compost. You can follow these steps for a leaf bin or a ny single-unit model.

Let's Do It →

1
First, remove any unfinished material from the top of the pile. Shovel (or pitchfork) the material into 5-gallon buckets or a wheelbarrow. This step is the least fun of the whole process because this material can be partially rotted and usually contains a fair number of squiggly decomposers. If the thought of seeing maggots eating your food grosses you out (no problem, I don't judge), freeze your food scraps and do not add them to your compost bin for a few weeks before harvest. Also, consider implementing the two-bin system in the next section.

2
Once you have cleared away the food scraps and undecomposed material, you will start to hit the brown gold. At this point, if your particular compost bin can lift up and off the pile, pick it up and move it out of the way. Shoveling

from the side of an exposed pile offers much better ergonomics than shoveling out of the top of the bin. After you lift the bin off, the compost inside holds its shape like you were molding a sand castle on the beach. Practically, this may require a little shaking and work to lift, especially if you only harvest once per year.

3
Now that you have your finished compost exposed, shovel the treasure into a wheelbarrow and admire. Keep an eye out for large sticks or pieces not quite finished decomposing and pull them out of the finished compost.

4
Once you have harvested all the finished compost, place the bin back in place and restart your pile with the scraps you removed in Step 1 and the pieces you pulled out while harvesting. Bury any food scraps with leaves.

This single-unit bin composts food scraps and leaves from a family a four.

If you purchased a plastic compost bin, you may have a little access door in the bottom of your bin that the manufacturer intended for harvesting. In my experience, this little door does not make harvesting easier. Sometimes, if you need just a few shovels of compost, you can open this door and pull out what you need. However, when you want to harvest a whole compost bin full of material, trying to dig all the material out of this door feels like trying to move a mountain with a spoon. Moving the whole bin out of your way to expose the compost proves much more efficient.

If you made the DIY Garbage Can Composter in Chapter 5, I recommend starting your compost harvest by pulling the can out of the ground. This may require some gentle turning from side to side to dislodge it from the surrounding soil. Since a full compost container may weigh quite a bit, ask for help dumping the material. Just as described above, dump the unfinished material first. Then empty the finished material into a wheelbarrow, into a pile on the ground, or straight onto a garden bed. Set the can back down into the ground and begin the process again.

The More the Merrier: Why You May Want Two Bins

Maintaining two compost bins provides many benefits if you can afford the space in your yard. If you have two bins, you can fill one up and allow the materials to compost while you fill up the second unit. You still need to aerate and check the moisture level of the first bin, but when harvest time comes around, you have a full bin of finished compost that requires little to no sorting.

Create a two-bin system simply by purchasing two compost bins instead of one. Or when you build a unit, construct two corrals instead of one. If the thought of shoveling squishy old melons full of maggots makes you scrunch your nose, I highly recommend the two-bin method. You can appreciate your macroinvertebrate friends from a distance without feeling the need to strike up a conversation.

Some very sophisticated gardeners may even have three-bin composting units. They add materials to one unit and have the material in the second and third units at varying stages of finishing decomposition. If you have a very large garden and need to process a great deal of material, consider a three-unit compost system. Harvesting material from a three-bin unit only requires pulling finished material from the oldest pile.

Having two compost bins allows this homeowner to add food scraps to one while the other finishes composting.

This tumbler has a twist-off end for easy access.

Harvesting Compost from a Tumbler

Unless your model of compost tumbler has two compartments, you will face an issue similar to single-unit composters: the need to separate unfinished compost from finished. Use the tumbler's fast composting to your advantage and do not add compostables for three weeks to a month before harvesting. You could freeze these food scraps (label the containers well or your family may create smoothies from less-than-desirable scraps) and set aside yard trimmings for that period.

Finished compost from a tumbler will smell sweet and earthy and no longer resemble the original material, with the exception of sticks and other woody debris. Shovel the material out of the tumbler and into a wheelbarrow or bucket. Compost from a tumbler will continue to mature after you integrate the material into your garden.

The Life-Changing Experience of Screening Compost

I never used to screen my harvested compost. It seemed like a waste of time when I could simply shovel out the finished compost and spread it around my garden. Why mess with an extra step?

Most composting is a waiting game. You spend months adding food scraps, leaves, and other material to the bin, turning the pile, and checking the moisture level. But when the process is complete, you have the satisfaction of pulling out shovelfuls of brown gold. Screening elevates that satisfaction to a whole new level, transforming your backyard compost into something you would pay top dollar for at a garden store, only better, because this compost is your creation.

You just have to experience the feeling for yourself. Sometimes I will stand back with a satisfied grin just admiring my full wheelbarrow of beautiful, dark-brown crumbly goodness. You should feel proud. You made this compost out of what some people consider to be garbage.

Sometimes specialty garden stores will sell compost screens, and you can find a few outlets online. Compost screens resemble the devices old-fashioned miners used when panning for gold, only our gold filters through, leaving the undecomposed bits on top. The easiest-to-use compost screens can stretch across a wheelbarrow so your finished compost filters right into the bucket of the wheelbarrow. Screen with ½-inch holes provides large enough openings for compost to sift down while still screening material out. Smaller mesh will suffice but may require more work to push the desired material through.

Work the compost back and forth across the screen crumbling clumps as needed.

Place large pieces left behind on the screen back into the compost bin.

Screening compost requires only three easy steps:

1. Place your screener over a wheelbarrow or bucket.

2. Plop a shovelful of compost on top and move the material back and forth. I prefer to do this with gloved hands so I can rescue any worms from the compost screen guillotine.

3. Throw anything too large to go through the screen back into the compost pile for further decomposition.

Screening compost proves easiest with relatively dry compost rather than mushy and mud-like compost. If you have compost on the squishier side, consider setting it out on the ground or a tarp to dry for a day. Drier compost will clump less and break apart easily as you screen.

Unless you practice incredible meticulousness when adding materials, you may encounter non-organic items as you screen your compost. These could include plastic identification tags from plants, pantyhose used to tie staked tomatoes, produce stickers, or the occasional random toy (if you have kids like mine). Needless to say, pull these out and reuse or throw away as desired.

The Toughest Compostables

MOST OF THE MATERIALS added to your compost will end up indistinguishable from each other. The banana peel and apple core look identical when decomposed. Some of our compostables, however, possess a stubborn streak, and we will find them in finished compost.

Eggshells are the most obvious material in screened compost. These usually break into tiny bits but decompose very slowly, resulting in finished compost with many shards of eggshell. If this look bothers you, you have two options. First, simply don't compost eggshells. Second, grind the eggshells up into a powder. As you can imagine, grinding eggshells is a time-intensive activity requiring you to dirty up a blender or other chopping device.

I kind of like the look and know a secret benefit of eggshells in your compost when used as mulch: supposedly, eggshells deter slugs because the shards slice at the slugs' bellies when they come to enjoy your plants. While this might seem like a particularly cruel and unusual form of torture, anyone working to eliminate pests without using pesticides should appreciate the value of deterring slugs.

Other compostables you will find as you screen include mango seeds, avocado pits, shells from nuts, and tough, woody debris. Toss these back into your bin to continue decomposing. If you do not screen and they end up integrated in your garden, they will just finish their decomposition in place.

Eggshells are the last scrap to decompose in compost, but they will help deter slugs from eating your plants.

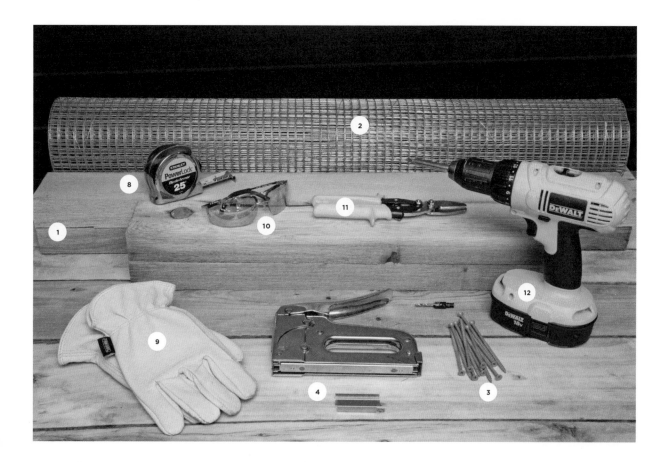

DIY COMPOST SCREENER

Since you may have a hard time finding a good compost screen (and the price will have you raising your eyebrows when you do find them), most composters make their own screens. The process is easy and requires little more than an hour and some basic supplies. Screeners comprise a simple box with a screen attached. Should you desire to get fancy, you can add some handles to the sides.

If you have any scrap lumber lying around, this project would make great use of your extra materials. You can use any type of wood, but cedar and treated lumber will hold up the longest. We used cedar and hardware cloth left over from building a compost bin.

Materials Needed:

1 2 × 4 lumber, (2) 48″, (2) 21″
2 2′ × 2′ galvanized ½″ hardware cloth
3 Galvanized #10 screws, (12) 4″
4 Staple gun and ½″ staples
5 *Screwdriver*
6 *Saw (handsaw or circular power saw)*
7 *Hammer*
8 Tape measure
9 Gloves
10 Safety glasses
11 Aviation shears
12 Drill

 Pictured   *Not shown*

Let's Do It ➜

1

If you are using a fresh piece of lumber, cut the 2 × 4 board into two 48″ pieces and two 21″ pieces. If you are using scrap lumber, try to find pieces that roughly match those lengths. The idea for this screener is for the length to rest across a wheelbarrow so the inner box hovers above the bucket of the wheelbarrow. As long as your pieces can lie across a wheelbarrow, the length is fine.

2
Set up your square by placing the smaller boards 12" from the ends of the long boards. The outside of the square should measure 24".

3
Connect the longer boards to the shorter boards using several screws drilled from the outside of the long boards. Secure at all four corners of the square.

4
Attach the hardware cloth to the outside of the square using a staple gun. Hammer in staples if needed. Hardware cloth can have sharp ends, so wear gloves and be sure to leave no pieces hanging over the edges to snag your clothes or skin. Screening compost should not be a bloody experience.

The design of this compost screener creates a basket to corral the compost while you work it back and forth. With a little creativity, you can modify these instructions to use the lumber you have. Creating a screener that spans the width of your wheelbarrow will save you time when you harvest your compost. Simply shovel a scoop of compost on top, work the compost back and forth with your hands, and marvel at the amazingly beautiful material left underneath.

Using Your Finished Compost

Now that you have harvested your treasure, you have the fun of deciding how to use it. Unless you composted with an integrated method that left the compost in place, you can choose to cart your compost anywhere in your garden. I tend to spread the love around when I use compost, but your needs may differ from mine.

Consider all the areas in your garden. Do you have any underperforming beds that could use a little lift? Is your grass a little patchy or discolored and in need of some fertilizer? Are some of your beds lacking a fresh coating of mulch? The answers to these questions will lead you to some uses over others.

Mulch for Beds

Finished compost, particularly if you took the time to screen the compost, works well as a mulch in garden beds. You may discover that you want to display your prized creation in the most visible beds in your garden. Simply sprinkle the screened compost around plants as you would hardwood mulch.

This application mirrors what happens to decomposing material in nature. When plants and animals die in a forest (or desert, or prairie, or ocean), they decompose on the ground and then become the top layer of the forest floor (or whatever habitat in which they happen to die). Worms, other decomposers, and rainwater pull the nutrients down into the earth. This natural humus layer builds up over time.

A few inches of finished screened compost will beautify your garden, amend the soil, and provide shade for the soil underneath. Applying compost in this way helps the soil underneath retain water and maintain a healthy and diverse profile of soil life. If mulching around trees or shrubs, leave a few inches of gap between the compost and the bark so you do not start composting the tree.

Testing Your Soil

YOU KNOW by now (if you have been paying attention) that compost provides a myriad of benefits as a soil amendment. It improves the soil's ability to retain water when needed and release water when needed. The macroorganisms present in the finished compost help plants take in necessary nutrients. The compost itself can provide much-needed nutrients. The question becomes what does your soil need?

Depending on what plants you plant and the type of soil you have, your soil could need a number of different amendments. The pH could measure low or high, the minerals could be low, or your soil could have a less-than-desirable percentage of organic materials. You never know until you test your soil. Most local agricultural extension agencies offer kits to test your soil, or you can purchase a kit online. A soil test will make recommendations on what your soil lacks so you can add the best supplements. Even with all its superpowers, sometimes your soil may need more than just compost.

Amending Soil

When you have a new garden bed or very poor soil, working the compost down into the soil will help improve the humus and topsoil layers, drainage, and nutrient availability. The process of amending soil with compost looks like you would imagine. Dump some compost on top of the soil and work it in with a shovel (or tiller if you have one). Amend the soil when the ground is not too wet and you will save your back muscles the extra work.

As you integrate the compost into the soil, remember that plants need the minerals from the soil as well. Planting straight into compost usually does not work. Generally, you want to add 2 to 4 inches of compost for every 6 inches of soil. Use your judgement based on the quality of your soil and how much compost you have to go around.

Make Potted Plants Happier

You can also make use of your compost in potted plants, both indoors and outdoors. In more compact space, you will want to ensure that the ratio of compost to potting soil is more exact than when you amend soil on the ground. Too much compost in a pot could burn the roots or kill the plant. On the other hand, the right amount of compost in a pot will give you the most amazing patio tomatoes you have ever seen.

When potting plants, you want to mix one part compost to every two parts potting soil. Mix the two materials together before adding the plant to the pot. Water the plant well and relax. Depending on the type of plant you potted, the compost may provide the plant with all the fertilizer it needs.

If the plant is indoors, you may want to pasteurize the soil to avoid any diseases to which indoor plants are more susceptible. To pasteurize the soil, simple sprinkle the soil on a baking pan and place it in a 200°F oven for 1 hour. Allow to cool before you plant your indoor plants.

Mix one part compost to every two parts potting soil when potting a new plant.

Seed Starter

Many gardeners want to provide their most delicate plants, otherwise known as seedlings, the benefit of finished compost. Aside from amending the soil, you can use a mixture of finished compost and vermiculite to cover seeds after you plant them. Vermiculite adds lightness to the compost that allows small seedlings to push through to the surface.

Mix compost and vermiculite in equal parts and spread it over seeds at the depth required for that plant.

Lawns Want Compost Too

We already discussed in detail the merits of grasscycling (see Chapter 6), but sometimes your lawn needs more of a boost (or sometimes all you have is a lawn with no garden beds). You can use compost to fertilize your lawn and amend the sometimes-neglected soil underneath.

As a topdressing, compost will work its way between the blades and amend the soil supporting your grass. Screened compost works best because it has a fine texture. Dry compost will also distribute more easily into the grass. Simply spread about ¼ inch of fine-textured compost across the lawn. Use a leaf rake or a push broom (talk about raising your neighbors' eyebrows) to work the compost into the blades. Water your lawn to further encourage the compost to dissolve and amend the soil. Wait a week to mow, giving gravity time to pull the compost down to the soil.

If you want to overachieve, consider aerating your lawn before you apply the compost. Many home improvement stores will rent a core aerator to punch 2- to 3-inch holes throughout your lawn. These holes provide air and nutrients to the roots of your lawn. If you aerate before applying the compost, the compost will find its way into those holes and down into soil to amend it more easily.

Growing Mushrooms in Compost

Delicious fresh mushrooms are one of my top-five favorite foods. Just thinking of perfectly sautéed baby portabellas with golden brown edges in a buttery sauce makes my mouth water. When I learned that people actually grow their own mushrooms at home, I felt like a whole new world opened up to me. You too can grow edible, delicious mushrooms at home; many mushroom varieties love to grow in crumbly, moist compost.

I once took a class on growing your own mushrooms, and one quote from the speaker stuck with me: "All mushrooms are edible at least once." You have to be very careful, because some mushrooms possess chemicals creating psychedelic effects that could cause permanent brain damage, and other varieties could kill you.

But we are not talking about foraging the forest for mushrooms. We are talking about gardening your own mushrooms in a contained environment using finished compost and purchased spores. You need to take a few basic precautions when using compost and growing your own mushrooms. First, you need to find a source of mushroom spores. Several companies online sell these, and of course, I would strongly recommend going with a reputable company and not borrowing some spores from your hippie neighbor who spends a little too much time in his basement.

Most reputable sources of spores can tell you which mushrooms are easier to grow and which like compost as a growing medium. Oyster, button, and shiitake all seem to grow easily for beginners, but button mushrooms prefer compost over other mediums. When you purchase mushroom spawn, you receive a mixture of mushroom spores (the microscopic cells responsible for spreading the fungus) and the ingredients the mushrooms need to thrive.

Aside from a reputable source for your mushroom spawn, follow all of the spore source's suggestions for preparing the compost so you do not accidently cultivate a fungus existing in the compost and eat the wrong mushroom. Some serious mushroom growers create a specialized compost just for growing the type of mushroom they desire.

Raised Beds Love Compost

Whether you have existing raised beds you want to amend or you plan to construct new raised beds, your finished compost has your back. If you have an existing raised bed, spread about 2 inches of compost over the bed in the fall and then cover it with mulch. The mulch and the compost will protect the soil over the winter. You can also amend the soil in the spring with finished compost before planting as a layer on top for the no-till method or worked into the soil.

Constructing a new raised bed will use more compost. Most experienced gardeners recommend a mix of 60 percent topsoil, 30 percent compost, and 10 percent potting mix. Thoroughly mixing these three materials before planting should provide a nice starting material for your plants. Raised beds, though often open at the bottom, follow similar rules as potting plants with compost. Add the compost carefully to make sure you do not add so much that you deprive your plants of the important minerals in soil.

Incorporating finished compost into raised beds improves the soil environment for your plants.

Brewing Compost Tea

Often, we wish the benefits of our compost could stretch farther across our gardens. If you find yourself looking around feeling like you have more plants in need of compost than you have compost, consider following a tip from serious composters: brew some compost tea. Compost tea transforms compost into a liquid fertilizer, spreading the compost love to more of your plants. It provides soluble nitrogen and beneficial microorganisms to your plants immediately, and the process, while more complicated than applying compost as a soil amendment, is easier than brewing your own beer.

When you make compost tea, your goal is to encourage the beneficial bacteria living in your compost to multiply like crazy over a short period of time. Plants love these bacteria, so providing a boost of the bacteria to your plants will help them absorb more nutrients. The combination of the sugar in the molasses and the aeration from the aquarium pump help fuel the explosion of beneficial bacteria.

You must use completely decomposed compost when making the compost tea, or you could end up with some weird fermented food scrap moonshine not fit for drinking or applying to plants. Many vermicomposters choose this method since vermicomposting results in a relatively small quantity of finished compost compared to backyard composting. Most compost tea brewers use found or pieced-together setups with a hodge-podge of materials that look less than impressive but work just as well as the fancy sets available online.

Strawberries Thrive in Compost Socks

MANY PLANTS like compost, but none are quite as red, sweet, and tempting as strawberries. Strawberries need well-drained soil in which to grow, or they could face black root rot. Compost offers the perfect solution, providing an ideal growing medium for the little red fruits. Since strawberries like well-drained soil, many gardeners plant them in mounds or in raised beds. Incorporate at least 2 inches of compost in the top 6 inches of soil.

Some gardeners even create compost "tubes" or "socks" using cotton or burlap mesh to grow strawberries. You can purchase compost socks or make your own. Fill an 8-inch-diameter tube with compost. Make the tube as long as you need, but most are between 3 and 6 feet long. Lay it on top of the soil and slit the tube every 8 inches to plant a strawberry plant in each slit. Install a drip irrigation system nearby and watch the strawberries thrive. The USDA has shown that compost socks significantly reduce the occurrence of black root rot and increase fruit yields 16 to 32 fold.

DIY COMPOST TEA RECIPE

Materials Needed:

1 5-gallon bucket or old plastic cat litter bucket
2 Aquarium pump
3 2 tablespoons sulfur-free molasses
4 Pantyhose (creates a "tea bag" for the compost)
5 Approximately 4 to 5 cups of finished compost (about 1 shovelful)
6 Watering can

1
First, fill the bucket within a few inches of the top with water. If the water is chlorinated, give it a few hours for the chlorine to evaporate.

2
Place the finished compost into the pantyhose and push it down to the toe area. The pantyhose acts as a bag to hold the compost but still allows water to penetrate, just like a tea bag.

3
Place the compost tea bag into the water.

4
Add about 2 tablespoons of molasses to the bucket and stir.

5
Place the aerating part of the aquarium pump into the bucket and weigh it down with rocks if necessary. Turn on the pump.

6
Give the compost tea about 24 hours to brew.

7
You should see a frothy top on the compost tea 24 hours later. Pour the mixture into a watering can and dilute it 1:1 with the dechlorinated water, if desired.

pantyhose filled with compost

Air stones

Aquarium pump

Brewing compost tea requires only a few basic materials and takes less than a day. The resulting liquid acts like a fertilizer for your plants.

If you do not have an aquarium pump, you can mix the compost every 20 minutes for 3 hours. A garden stake or other long tool works well for this purpose. Your goal in stirring is to completely aerate the liquid, so do not hold back in your aggressive stirring. Honestly, aquarium pumps are cheap, so unless some hands-on repetitive stirring sounds like fun to you, I recommend throwing $10 down on an aquarium pump. You can also omit the molasses in the recipe and still end up with some nice compost tea.

After you have finished making the tea, you can use the leftover material in the pantyhose as a soil amendment to add humus material to your garden. If you want to scale up this process and brew a large amount of compost tea, you could use a garbage can or a 30-gallon plastic drum and increase the recipe accordingly. If you do scale up, consider how you will remove the compost tea from the container. A spout or spigot near the bottom of the container will allow you to fill up a watering can. Place the spout at least 6 inches from the bottom so any settling compost does not clog up the drain.

I am certain I do not need to say this, but as a disclaimer, *do not drink this tea*. Even with 2 tablespoons of molasses, it will taste like dirt. Literally.

Obsessed Yet?

Even before you harvest your first shovelful of beautiful, crumbly compost, you may develop a bit of an obsession with composting. It is hard not to fall in love with an activity that improves your soil, benefits the environment, saves you money, and gets you outside. If you are not already, you will be scolding your spouse for throwing out a banana peel or inventing new ways to steal your neighbor's brown paper bag of leaves.

If you have a deep desire to learn more about backyard composting, I highly recommend you check to see if a nearby garden center or local government office offers a Master Composter class in your area. These intensive classes cover many of the topics you already learned in this book but also offer hands-on demonstrations and supply you with a network of people in your area who are as crazy about composting as you are. Also, when was the last time you could call yourself a master of anything?

So many people tell me in the hushed tone of a confession that they actually like composting more than they like gardening. I feel the same way. Composting is so practical and useful. You take your leftovers and give back to the soil, replicating nature. Once you have a feeling for balancing the browns and the greens, memorize your list of acceptable and unacceptable materials, and work aerating and watering the pile into your routine, composting becomes second nature. It is hard to imagine a time when I routinely threw away those banana peels and coffee grounds.

I hope this book has provided you the inspiration and knowledge you need to start successfully composting in your own backyard. Rest assured, composting has a forgiving nature, and no matter how many mistakes you make along the way, compost happens. The materials you add will decompose and turn into a valuable soil amendment in the end. Happy composting!

Acknowledgments

This book would not have been possible without the support, knowledge, and passion of many family and friends. My husband, Adam, offered his knowledge of tools and construction, spent countless hours constructing the bins in this book and preparing for photo shoots, and kept the kids entertained (or at least out of the way) so I could write. Dalton Stockton built the most beautiful compost bin I have ever seen and lent his carpentry expertise to give all our projects a polished look. Joy and George Balz and Dodie and Rick Stockton allowed us access to their homes and yards for photo shoots and provided free childcare in the process. John Barlage, my pickle barrel hero, not only found a local company selling used pickle barrels, but picked one up and delivered it to me without even being asked. Holly Utrata-Halcomb with the Hamilton County Soil and Water Conservation District conducted the fascinating study on the varied results of backyard composting. Akiko and Imu Aloway, Kelly Fogwell, Dalton and Elliot Stockton, Adam Balz, Nid and Josie Balz, Ben and Emily Balz, Gary Dangel, and June Stockton all patiently modeled for photos. Gary Dangel built a beautiful African keyhole garden and introduced me to the idea of Hugelkultur. Kathy Fogwell, Megan Hummel, Sharon Brotherton, Jenny Lohmann, Ron Herrmann, Julie Beaulieu, Christina Tenhundfeld, Belinda Frykman, Samantha Smith, Charlie Gonzalez, MaryEllen Etienne (my favorite reuse warrior), Mary Dudley, and Kylie Johnson offered suggestions, expertise, and input. Alex and Nid Balz gave use access to their beautiful urban yard for photos of the tumbler assembly. John Duke bestowed his wealth of composting knowledge and experience and gave me a library of composting references. The Civic Garden Center of Greater Cincinnati allowed Anna and me to use their beautiful grounds for photos and provided valuable connections to local gardeners. Several lovely neighbors in the communities of Clifton and Northside allowed us to photograph their compost bins. Last but not least, Anna Stockton shared her amazing photography skills in this book (I knew you would capture the beauty of composting).

Bibliography and Reference List

BOOKS

Appelhof, Mary. *Worms Eat My Garbage.* Kalamazoo, MI: Flower Press, 1997.

BioCycle. *The BioCycle Guide to the Art and Science of Composting.* Emmaus, PA: The JG Press, 1991.

Campbell, Stu. *Let It Rot! The Gardener's Guide to Composting.* Pownal, VT: Storey Communications, 1998.

Gilliard, Spring. *Diary of a Compost Hotline Operator.* Cabriola Island, BC: New Society Publishers, 2003.

McDowell, C. Forrest, and Tricia Clark-McDowell. *Home Composting Made Easy.* Eugene, OR: Cortesia Press, 1998.

Minnich, Jerry, and Marjorie Hunt. *The Rodale Guide to Composting.* Emmaus, PA: Rodale Press, 1979.

Overgaard, Karen, and Tony Novembre. *The Composting Cookbook.* Toronto: Greenline Products, 2002.

Pleasant, Barbara, and Deborah L. Martin. *The Complete Compost Gardening Guide.* North Adams, MA: Storey Publishing, 2008.

Arsenault, Chris. "Only 60 Years of Farming Left if Soil Degradation Continues." *Scientific American* (2017). www.scientificamerican.com/article/only-60-years-of-farming-left-if-soil-degradation-continues

Brantley, Elizabeth A., Donald D. Davis, and Larry J. Kuhns. "What Is Growing in My Landscape Mulch? Mushrooms, Slime Molds, Bird's Nest Fungus, Artillery Fungus." PennState Extension (2009). www.extension.psu.edu/publications/ul201

"Compost Fundamentals, Compost Benefits and Uses." Washington State University, Whatcom County Extension. http://whatcom.wsu.edu/ag/compost/fundamentals/benefits_benefits.htm

Dickson, Nancy, Thomas Richard, and Robert Kozlowski. *Composting to Reduce the Waste Stream: A Guide to Small Scale Food and Yard Waste Composting.* Northeast Regional Agricultural Engineering Service, 1991. ecommons.cornell.edu/handle/1813/44736

Funt, Richard C., and Jane Martin. "Black Walnut Toxicity to Plants, Humans, and Horses." Ohio State University Extension (2015). www.berkeley.ext.wvu.edu/r/download/211509

Hamilton County Recycling and Solid Waste District. *Confessions of a Composter* (blog). www.confessionsofacomposter.blogspot.com

Cornell Waste Management Institute. Cornell University. www.cwmi.css.cornell.edu/chapter3.pdf

Eliades, Angelo. "Deep Green Permaculture." deepgreenpermaculture.com/diy-instructions/hot-compost-composting-in-18-days/

Feiger, Judith. "Make a Compost Bin from a Trash Can." *Mother Earth News* (September/October 1976). www.motherearthnews.com/organic-gardening/make-a-compost-bin-zmaz76soztak

Glausiusz, Josie. "Is Dirt the New Prozac?" *Discover* (July 2007). www.discovermagazine.com/2007/jul/raw-data-is-dirt-the-new-prozac

Hoitink, Henry A. J., and Ligia Zuniga De Ramos. *Disease Suppression with Compost: History, Principles, and Future.* Ohio Agriculture Research and Development Center, Ohio State University. Wooster, OH.

"The Many Benefits of Hugelkultur." *Inspiration Green and Permaculture* (October 17, 2013). www.permaculture.co.uk/articles/many-benefits-hugelkultur

Millner, Patricia. "Socking It to Strawberry Root Rot." *Agriculture Research* (September 2007). www.agresearchmag.ars.usda.gov/2007/sep/root

Natural Resources Defense Council and the Ad Council. Save the Food. www.savethefood.com

Platt, Brenda, James McSweeney, and Jenn Davis. *Growing Local Fertility: A Guide to Community Composting.* Highfields Center for Composting and the Institute for Local Self-Reliance (April 2014). www.ilsr.org/wp-content/uploads/2014/07/growing-local-fertility.pdf

Project Groundwork, Metropolitan Sewer District of Greater Cincinnati. www.projectgroundwork.org

Rowell, Brent, and Robert Hadad. "Organic Manures and Fertilizers for Vegetable Crops." University of Kentucky Department of Horticulture (2017).

Schwartz, Judith D. "Soil as Carbon Storehouse: New Weapon in Climate Fight?" *Yale Environment 360* (March 4, 2014). www.e360.yale.edu/features/soil_as_carbon_storehouse_new_weapon_in_climate_fight

Trautmann, Nancy. "Invertebrates of the Compost Pile." Cornell Composting Science and Engineering (1996). www.compost.css.cornell.edu/invertebrates.html

University of Illinois Extension. "History of Composting." *Composting for the Homeowner* (blog) (2017). web.extension.illinois.edu/homecompost/history.cfm

US Composting Council. *Compost and Its Benefits.* (2008). www.compostingcouncil.org/wp/wp-content/uploads/2015/06/compost-and-its-benefitsupdated2015.pdf

US Environmental Protection Agency. "Advancing Sustainable Materials Management: Facts and Figures." (2013). www.epa.gov/smm/advancing-sustainable-materials-management-facts-and-figures-report

———. "Municipal Solid Waste Generation, Recycling, and Disposal in the United States: Facts and Figures for 2012." www.epa.gov/sites/production/files/2015-09/documents/2012_msw_fs.pdf

———. "Overview of Greenhouse Gases." (2017). www.epa.gov/ghgemissions/overview-greenhouse-gases

Waltz, Clint, and Becky Griffin. "Grasscycling: Let the Clippings Fall Where They May." University of Georgia Cooperative Extension (June 18, 2013). www.extension.uga.edu/publications/detail.cfm?number=C1031

Appendix A

WHICH COMPOSTING STYLE IS RIGHT FOR YOU?

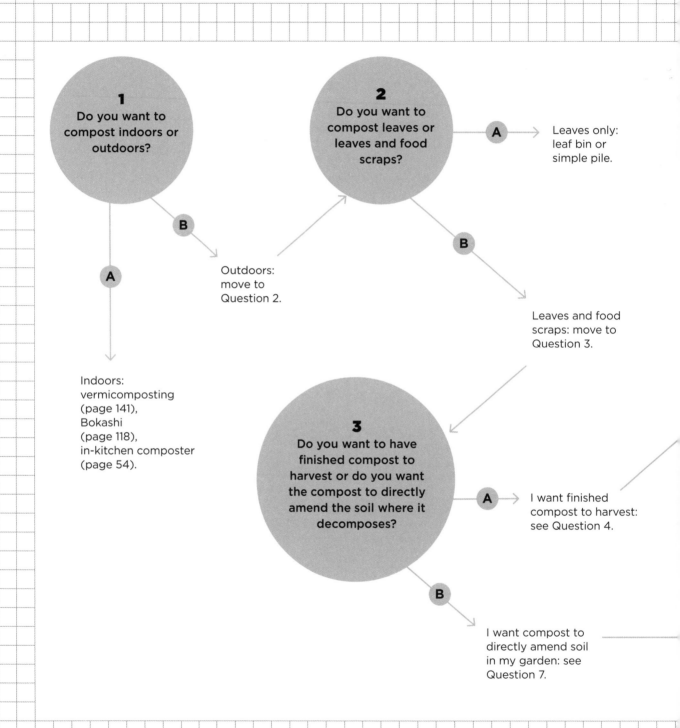

1 Do you want to compost indoors or outdoors?

2 Do you want to compost leaves or leaves and food scraps?

A Leaves only: leaf bin or simple pile.

B Outdoors: move to Question 2.

B Leaves and food scraps: move to Question 3.

A Indoors: vermicomposting (page 141), Bokashi (page 118), in-kitchen composter (page 54).

3 Do you want to have finished compost to harvest or do you want the compost to directly amend the soil where it decomposes?

A I want finished compost to harvest: see Question 4.

B I want compost to directly amend soil in my garden: see Question 7.

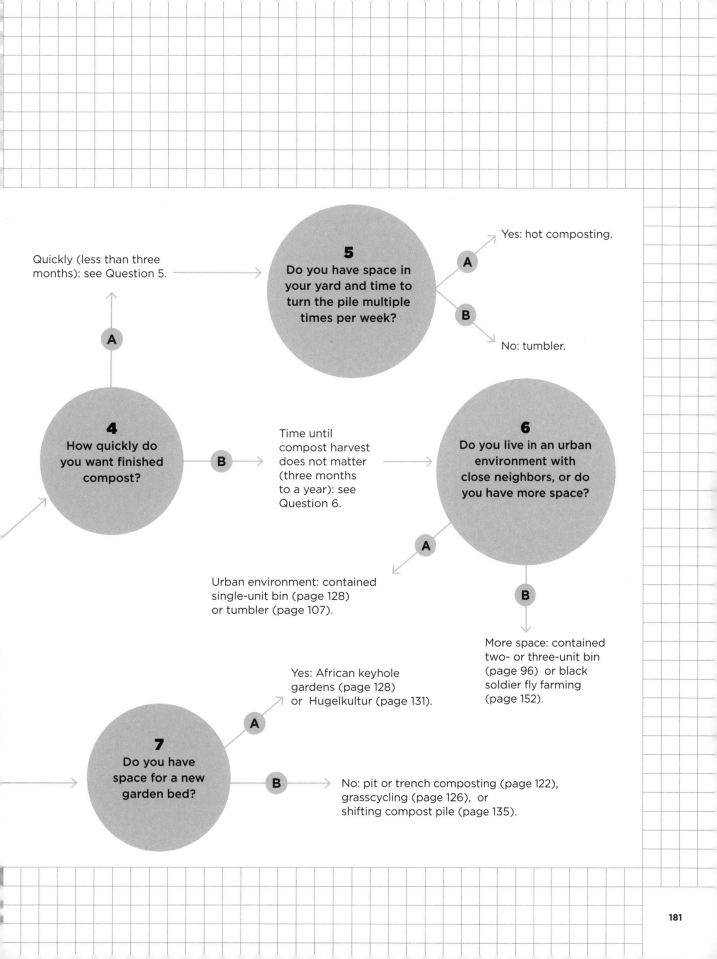

Quickly (less than three
months): see Question 5. ----->

5
**Do you have space in
your yard and time to
turn the pile multiple
times per week?**

A Yes: hot composting.

B No: tumbler.

4
**How quickly do
you want finished
compost?**

B Time until
compost harvest
does not matter
(three months
to a year): see
Question 6.

6
**Do you live in an urban
environment with
close neighbors, or do
you have more space?**

A Urban environment: contained
single-unit bin (page 128)
or tumbler (page 107).

B More space: contained
two- or three-unit bin
(page 96) or black
soldier fly farming
(page 152).

7
**Do you have
space for a new
garden bed?**

A Yes: African keyhole
gardens (page 128)
or Hugelkultur (page 131).

B No: pit or trench composting (page 122),
grasscycling (page 126), or
shifting compost pile (page 135).

Appendix B

Compost Recipes

SUGGESTED HOT COMPOST RECIPE

INGREDIENTS:

6 parts dry shredded leaves

3 parts shredded newspaper or straw

1 part manure or coffee grounds

1 part fresh grass clippings or yard trimmings

1 part food scraps (chopped small)

1 shovelful good finished compost

METHOD:

Place the straw on the bottom. Layer the green and brown materials. Place most of the food scraps on the bottom layers and near the center of the pile. Add a shovelful of finished compost halfway through layers. Turn the pile frequently according to the hot composting guidelines on page 75.

SUGGESTED SIMPLE WIRE LEAF BIN RECIPE

INGREDIENTS:

10 parts shredded leaves

1 part coffee grounds

METHOD:

Layer the coffee grounds in with the leaves for faster decomposition. Water the bin if you experience dry weather for more than two weeks.

SUGGESTED GARBAGE CAN COMPOSTER RECIPE

INGREDIENTS:

1 shovelful mulch, wood chips, or straw

3 parts shredded leaves

1 part food scraps

METHOD:

Place the mulch, wood chips, or straw on the bottom of the composter. Add the food scraps and cover them with leaves. Continue adding food scraps and covering them, using a 1 part food scraps to 3 parts shredded leaves ratio.

SUGGESTED TWO-UNIT COMPOSTER RECIPE

INGREDIENTS:

6 parts shredded leaves

1 part food scraps or coffee grounds

1 part plant trimmings

METHOD:

Bury the food scraps under the leaves and add coffee grounds to the top of the pile to deter rodents. Add plant trimmings whenever available. Chop up larger pieces of plant trimmings so they "cook" faster. Water during dry weather so the pile is as wet as a wrung-out sponge.

SUGGESTED TUMBLER COMPOSTING RECIPE

INGREDIENTS:

2 parts finely shredded leaves

1 part shredded newspaper or cardboard

1 part food scraps

1 part weeds

1 shovelful good garden soil

METHOD:

Toss all the materials into the tumbler and turn. If the food scraps have a high water content or the compost materials look too wet, add dry shredded newspaper or cardboard as needed. Turn the tumbler weekly.

SUGGESTED SIMPLE COMPOST PILE RECIPE

INGREDIENTS:

3 parts brown leaves

1 part green yard trimmings

METHOD:

Pile the materials on the ground and wait.

SUGGESTED TRENCH COMPOSTING RECIPE

INGREDIENTS:

3 parts shredded leaves

1 part food scraps

1 cup of cottonseed meal, alfalfa meal, or blood meal per 20 pounds of material

METHOD:

Mix the food scraps and leaves into the trench. Dust the top with high-nitrogen meal such as alfalfa meal or blood meal. Cover with soil.

SUGGESTED AFRICAN KEYHOLE GARDEN RECIPE

INGREDIENTS:

6 parts straw or shredded leaves

1 part manure and bedding

1 part food scraps

1 part green plant trimmings

METHOD:

Layer the food scraps and other materials, ensuring that the food scraps are well buried. When the garden needs watering, water through the compost bin.

SUGGESTED HUGELKULTUR RECIPE

INGREDIENTS:

Mix of hardwood and softwood logs and branches, enough to fill a trench 1 to 2 feet deep

1 part vines, twigs, and other tough materials

1 part manure

1 part leaves or straw

Topsoil dug from the trench

METHOD:

Place hardwood and then softwood in the bottom of trench. Cover with twigs, vines, and other tough materials. Cover with manure, leaves, and straw. Top with at least 6 inches of topsoil.

SUGGESTED SHIFTING COMPOST PILE RECIPE

INGREDIENTS:

3 parts shredded leaves

1 part yard trimmings, cut small

1 part manure with bedding

METHOD:

Build the pile, mixing all three materials as evenly as possible. Turn every few weeks by shifting the pile to a new location.

SUGGESTED SHEET COMPOST RECIPE

INGREDIENTS:

1 part black-and-white newspaper or cardboard without tape or staples

3 parts shredded leaves

2 parts straw

1 part manure

1 part food scraps

1 part yard trimmings

1 to 2 parts finished compost

1 part mulch

METHOD:

Build the bottom layer with newspaper or cardboard. Place 8 to 12 inches of shredded leaves, straw, manure, food scraps, and yard trimmings over the bottom layer. Completely cover the area with finished compost and then mulch.

Index

About the Author

Michelle Balz is a longtime backyard composter with a passion for reducing our impact on the planet. She spends her days writing laid-back advice for home composters on her blog, *Confessions of a Composter*, teaching classes on backyard composting, and learning everything she can about composting, recycling, reusing, and waste reduction. Since 2002, Michelle has worked as a solid waste (a.k.a. garbage) professional, encouraging residents and businesses to reduce their waste and use fewer resources. Michelle has a bachelor's degree in Environmental Studies and a master's degree in Professional Writing both from the University of Cincinnati. She lives in Cincinnati, Ohio, with her high-school-sweetheart-turned-husband, Adam, and two adorable children, Benjamin and Emily.